'TICH' FREEMAN
and the Decline of
the Leg-Break Bowler

'TICH' FREEMAN

and the Decline of the Leg-Break Bowler

BY DAVID LEMMON

London
GEORGE ALLEN & UNWIN
Boston   Sydney

George Allen & Unwin (Publishers) Ltd,
40 Museum Street, London WC1A 1LU, UK

George Allen & Unwin (Publishers) Ltd,
Park Lane, Hemel Hempstead, Herts HP2 4TE, UK

Allen & Unwin Inc.,
9 Winchester Terrace, Winchester, Mass 01890, USA

George Allen & Unwin Australia Pty Ltd,
8 Napier Street, North Sydney, NSW 2060, Australia

First published in 1982

British Library Cataloguing in Publication Data

Lemmon, David
  'Tich' Freeman and the decline of the leg-break bowler.
1. Freeman, A.P.   2. Cricket players – England
– Biography
I. Title
796.35'8'0924   GV915.F/
ISBN 0-04-796055-8

Set in 11 on 13 point Garamond by Red Lion Setters, London
and printed in Great Britain
by Billing and Sons Ltd, Guildford, London and Worcester

Leg-spinners pose problems much like love,
Requiring commitment, the taking of a chance.

Alan Ross

Contents

List of Illustrations

Preface

There are many people to thank for their help and encouragement in writing this book. Some have written me letters; others have engaged in casual conversations. All have been valuable.

In particular, I would like to thank Kent County Cricket Club who, through the secretary of the club, Mr Maurice Fenner, have given me so much generous assistance. Les Ames, Howard Levett, Brian Valentine, Jack Bryan and Doug Wright have given me hours of their time in reminiscing and I am deeply grateful. Their help was invaluable and their company a privilege and delight.

To one man I owe the greatest debt of all. Mr Bernard Simmonds, assistant secretary of Kent C.C.C. and lover of the game, has provided me with every possible help. He has loaned me documents and answered my every query. Please accept my thanks.

David Lemmon

Introduction

On the late afternoon of 3 June 1980, Leicestershire were poised for their first victory of the season. They had bowled Derbyshire out for 118 in the second innings so that they needed 199 to win in two and a quarter hours. Balderstone, Birkenshaw and Gower had batted with great panache and they seemed to be moving easily to their target. Tolchard was the fifth man out with the score at 190, but when Gower slashed the last ball of the penultimate over for four it meant that Leicestershire needed only one to win off the last over.

The last over was bowled by Kim Barnett, who bowled only 55.3 overs in the whole of the season. The batsman was Tim Boon, a young player of considerable promise. Barnett bowled with commendable accuracy for a young man not yet 20 who was essentially a batsman and whose experience of first-class cricket was limited to just over one season. Boon was able to make nothing of the first five deliveries. He prodded the last ball of the match into the off-side field and scampered for what would have been the winning run, but Kirsten's throw beat him to the bowler's end and he was run out. The match had ended with the scores level and Leicestershire had to wait until August for their first victory of the season.

The event passed almost unnoticed for the news was dominated by Gooch's fifth century of the season, by Middlesex moving to the top of the Schweppes County Championship table, by the first Test match against the West Indies which was due to begin on the Thursday, and by the Derby Stakes run at Epsom on 4 June.

In its own way, however, that last over at Leicester was more

1

remarkable than any of these happenings. What made it significant was that it was bowled by Kim Barnett who is a leg-break bowler and, as such, is part of a species close to extinction. For his captain, Geoff Miller, to have allowed him to bowl that over was seen by some as an act of faith in a young player, by others as an act of lunacy. Barnett was one of only ten players who bowled leg-breaks in the English first-class season of 1980. It is worth examining the other nine.

Seven of them were batsmen who turned their arms only on occasions, mostly when a game was dead or when their captains wished to encourage the other side to score runs. 'Pasty' Harris, one-time opening batsman and occasional wicket-keeper, bowled for Nottinghamshire against Cambridge University, and Alastair Hignell bowled a couple of overs for Gloucestershire against Oxford University in the opening game of the season. Clive Radley, Keith Fletcher, Javed Miandad, Alvin Kallicharran and Sadiq Mohammad bowled very infrequently and in the contexts mentioned above. Fletcher, for example, conceded runs at nearly eight an over and Sadiq's one wicket cost 252 runs. Only two players, Robin Hobbs and Intikhab Alam, were front line bowlers.

Like Javed Miandad, Hobbs played for Glamorgan and when on one occasion they were operating together, it was reported: 'With leg-spin from both ends it was apparent that by now Glamorgan had conceded the match.'

In 1980, Hobbs was 38 years old. He had played for Essex from 1961 until 1975 when he had retired from first-class cricket. It was believed that he was somewhat disillusioned with the way in which the game was moving; he had played in every John Player League game one season without bowling a ball. A sensitive and affable man, he returned to the game as captain of Glamorgan in 1979, but the county floundered and he resigned from the leadership at the end of the season. He remained on the staff as a player but was used in only a few games in 1980, bowling a mere 114.3 overs in the season.

Intikhab Alam was a year older than Hobbs. He was not selected for the Surrey side at the beginning of the year, but some excellent

2

performances in the 2nd XI brought him back into contention for a first-team place. He had a successful season which culminated in his being preferred to Pocock in the Surrey team for the Gillette Cup Final. Intikhab was the only leg-break bowler to operate with any regularity during the English cricket season of 1980.

Hobbs played seven Tests for England between 1967 and 1971. As Christopher Martin-Jenkins remarks in his fine *Who's Who of Test Cricketers*, 'Hobbs would have been a typical county spinner if he had been born sixty years earlier. As it happened he was for much of his career unique'.

With his first ball in Test cricket Intikhab took the wicket of Australian opener Colin McDonald. In all he played for Pakistan 47 times between 1959 and 1977, captaining his country in 17 Tests.

By the summer of 1980, however, spin-bowling in Test cricket had been reduced to the barest minimum. The series between England and the West Indies was dominated entirely by pace. The West Indies simply permutated their five quick bowlers, Roberts, Holding, Garner, Croft and Marshall, and omitted the off-spinner Parry, very successful in the county games, from every Test. Richards and Kallicharran sent down a few perfunctory overs of slow bowling, but never in anger.

Rather like the tennis-player who, having the ball hit at him hard and fast, tries to return it twice as hard, England attempted to respond in kind and suffered in consequence. Peter Willey played in all five Tests against the West Indies and in the Centenary Test, but he was primarily a batsman and by no stretch of imagination could he be considered a bowler of international standard, nor was he used as one.

England played Derek Underwood, left-arm, in the second Test and John Emburey, off-break bowler, in the remaining three and in the Centenary Test. When the side to tour the West Indies was announced in September Emburey and Miller, together with Willey, were named as the spinners. There was no-one in the party who turned the ball from leg.

The England–West Indies series of 1980 served only to

3

underline what had happened in the series between Australia and West Indies a few months earlier where spin had been eclipsed.

Australia has long been the home of great leg-break bowlers. Mailey, Grimmett, O'Reilly, Benaud: the line is a distinguished one, and the leg-break bowler still operates with considerable success at State level. O'Keefe, Hourn and Holland all appeared for New South Wales in the Sheffield Shield in 1979–80. Sleep, heralded as an outstanding cricketer, remained a mainstay of the South Australian side which came close to capturing the Shield, and Jim Higgs of Victoria was the most destructive bowler in the country. He topped the Australian first-class bowling averages and on the last afternoon of the season he bowled Victoria to a remarkable and dramatic victory in Adelaide by which they retained the Sheffield Shield which his bowling had done much to earn them the previous season.

Higgs played in one Test match against the West Indies when, though not bowling at his best, he captured three wickets. He then played in one Test match against England, when he bowled only one over. He was selected for the Australian tour of Pakistan but withdrew from the party for somewhat ambiguous reasons, one of which was lack of fitness. His lack of fitness did not prevent him from bowling at his very best in the closing weeks of the season when the Australian party was performing in Pakistan.

The man who was generally preferred to Higgs in the Australian side was another Victorian, the slow left-arm bowler Ray Bright. Bright is a defensive bowler. He has rarely troubled the best batsmen with his turn for he neither flights the ball nor spins it with any venom. During the course of the Australian season, 1979–80, Bright took seven wickets. They cost him 63.85 runs each. Higgs' 41 wickets cost him 20.34 apiece, yet it was Bright who came to England for the Centenary Test. The Australian selectors adopted the same policy when they came to choose the side to tour England in 1981, Bright being preferred to the more hostile Higgs, Holland or Sleep.

With Chandrasekhar having passed from the Test scene and Indian emphasis placed more and more on the pace of Kapil Dev, even the strongest bastion of spin seemed threatened and the decline and fall of the leg-break bowler complete. The England selectors supported this view when, contrary to expectations, they named only two spinners, Emburey and Underwood, in their party of 17 to tour India and Sri Lanka in the winter of 1981.

In the English first-class season of 1980 ten leg-break bowlers between them had bowled fewer than 600 overs. Fifty years previously, in five Test matches between England and Australia, four leg-break bowlers, three English and one Australian, had sent down 650 overs.

In 1981 there were only eight bowlers who bowled leg-breaks, but they bowled twice the number of overs that had been bowled by leg-spinners the previous summer. The two main bowlers were Robin Hobbs and Intikhab Alam. Hobbs took 35 wickets in the 390.3 overs that he bowled, and Intikhab Alam took 65 wickets at a cost of 24.38 runs each in 560.5 overs. Both retired at the end of the season. Hobbs played his last game at Colchester where he took 5 for 85 against his old county. By coincidence, Intikhab's last game was also against Essex. He helped Surrey to an exciting victory on the last day of the season at The Oval. When he left the field to the applause of a small but enthusiastic crowd on 15 September, the first-class game in England was left without a single regular leg-spinner.

In the 1930 series referred to above, Clarrie Grimmett took 29 wickets, and his bowling, coupled with Bradman's magnificent batting, won Australia the rubber. The three English leg-break bowlers, Richard Tyldesley, Walter Robins and Ian Peebles finished in the first three places in the England bowling averages for the series.

By some fancy the greatest of leg-break bowlers was not chosen by the England selectors for any of the five Tests that summer though, in fact, he took ninety-six more wickets than any other bowler during the season. His total of 275 was eight more than it had been the previous season and one less than it would be the following season when, of course, he again took more wickets than any other bowler.

'Tich' Freeman

His name was Alfred Percy Freeman. He played for Kent and by 1930, he was forty-two years old. Because he was only five feet, two inches tall, he was known as 'Tich'.

1

The Golden Age

The leg-break bowler was born of an age which was essentially more joyful in its games than is ours. Although we assert the virtues of cricket, and the virtues that it inculcates, like all that is of human beings it is vulnerable and therefore corruptible. Cricket has not escaped the taint of materialism that has become the pre-occupation of the second half of the twentieth century.

A man who bowls out of the back of his hand, his fingers viciously turning the seam of the ball as he does so, is less likely to have complete control over the ball than any other type of bowler. If he is to master his art, he must throw the ball higher into the air than other bowlers and must experiment with the subtleties of flight. His stratagems are like those of the great chess-player. The chess-player may be forced to sacrifice his queen, his most valuable piece, in order to mate his opponent, and if the leg-break bowler concedes a few runs before the batsman falls into his trap, well so be it.

The philosophy of the Golden Age of cricket, that Edwardian twilight that preceded the first world war, accepted this, and the cricketers of the 'twenties and 'thirties saw little reason to challenge that philosophy.

In our times financial considerations and changing social habits and customs have bred limited-over cricket with its instant thrills and lack of subtlety. As the stakes have become higher, so acceptance of defeat has become less palatable. In limited-over cricket a match can be won without a wicket being taken. Containment is all and mediocre bowling, if it possesses the one virtue of accuracy, can prove more profitable than variety, subtlety, intelligence and experiment. Those who bowl slowly rarely attempt to spin the ball in limited-over cricket, preferring to nag away with low trajectory at a spot just outside the leg stump so that the batsman, seeing the leg-side field well guarded, forgets that he is playing a game of grace and beauty and backs away to leg in a grotesque effort to force the ball through the off-side. This is no game for the imaginative artist of spin and flight.

At the beginning of the century a young man from Oxford University, Bernard James Tindal Bosanquet, became tired of bowling fast-medium on artificial wickets and began to experiment with leg-break bowling. He added to his ability to bowl the leg-break a development of his own, the off-break bowled with what appeared to be the same action as the leg-break. It was a ball of cunning and deceit and it gave to the leg-break bowler a new and powerful weapon. The Australians were horrified when they first met it and called it the 'Bosie' after its inventor, but it became more commonly known as the googly.

It would be unwise to believe that Bosanquet was the first man ever to bowl a googly – Walter Mead of Essex had certainly done so – but it was Bosanquet who refined the delivery and made it a practical proposition. It is generally accepted that Bosanquet developed the googly by playing 'twisty-grab' over a billiard table. He then tried the patience of his friends for long hours in the nets before feeling confident enough to try it in a match. He introduced it successfully when playing for Middlesex and it became recognised as a potent weapon.

Bosanquet himself had one successful tour when his bowling at Sydney in the 1903–4 series won England the rubber. He bowled splendidly against Australia at Nottingham a year later, after which he drifted out of the game. His innovation had made a marked impression, however, and when the South Africans came to England in 1907 they included four googly bowlers in each of the three Tests.

It was Reggie Schwartz who had studied Bosanquet's methods and he instructed his colleagues. Schwartz himself bowled only the googly, but his disciples, Gordon White, Albert Vogler and Aubrey Faulkner, were leg-break and googly bowlers. England won the only Test that was decided, but the quartet of googly bowlers made a tremendous impression. It is worth remembering that Aubrey Faulkner, after a distinguished contribution as a soldier in the first world war, settled in England and opened a famous coaching school where he brought to the fore, among others, Ian Peebles and Doug Wright who was spotted there by Brian Valentine and taken down to Canterbury.

One reason for the stir caused by the South African quartet was that the googly was still not widely used in county cricket. The leg-break was, of course, by no means uncommon and the great S. F. Barnes, whose bowling defied any category, is said to have used it as his most devastating weapon. The googly was still shrouded in some mystery and enchantment and 'Father' Marriott tells how he and his school-friends in Ireland used to read avidly the illustrated articles on it which appeared in *The Captain* and *Pearsons Magazine*.

Spin-bowling in those years just before the first world war was mainly in the hands of the slow left-arm bowler. These were the great years of Wilfred Rhodes and Colin Blythe, and, for one memorable season, the annus mirabilis of W. C. 'Razor' Smith, quicker than the average spinner, who took 247 wickets in 1910.

Colin Blythe, upright and beautiful in all that he did, was the leading factor in Kent's first-ever Championship success in 1906, although a young man named Frank Woolley played his first games for the county that season. Blythe, so eloquently described by Harry Altham as 'a highly sensitive and nervous instrument beautifully co-ordinated, directed by a subtle mind, and inspired by a natural love of its art', gave his life in the first world war, but before then Kent had won three more Championships. Their second success came in 1909 and, although Blythe took 215 wickets that year, the most amazing contribution came from a bowler named Douglas Ward Carr who was playing in his first season of first-class cricket at the age of 37.

Carr had gone to school at Sutton Valence and from there to Brasenose College, Oxford. In 1891 he played in the Freshmen's match but, mainly due to a knee injury sustained while playing football, he played very little cricket at Oxford. He moved into club cricket in Kent, playing for Mote Park and the Band of Brothers. He had hovered between medium-pace bowling and the bowling of leg-breaks, and he became intrigued by the googly. He practised assiduously, but then discovered that he had lost the leg-break. By 1908 he had gained the ability to bowl both the leg-break and the googly and he was an outstanding success in club cricket. On 27, 28 and 29 May 1909 he made his first-class debut when he played for Kent against Oxford University at Oxford. He opened the bowling with Frank Woolley, took 5 for 65, and the University were bowled out for 125. He took two wickets in the second innings and Kent beat a not-very-strong Oxford side by an innings.

On the strength of this one performance Carr was invited to play for the Gentlemen against the Players both at The Oval and at Lord's. He had match figures of 8 for 138 in the first match and 7 for 128 in the second. He did not make his debut in the County Championship until 29 July when he played for Kent against Essex at Leyton where he returned match figures of 6 for 85. In seven Championship matches he took 51 wickets. He virtually won the game for Kent against Hampshire on the last day of Canterbury week when he dismissed Mead, Bowell, C. B. Fry, Capt. White and McDonell inside four overs.

He was in the England party for the fourth Test against Australia, but was omitted as the wicket was considered unfavourable to him. He was chosen for the fifth Test at The Oval, where he opened the bowling with Sydney Barnes. He bowled Gregory for one and then dismissed both Noble and Warwick Armstrong. MacLaren was severely criticised for his handling of Carr who was bowled into the ground and finished with 5 for 146. Although he dismissed Armstrong and Trumper in the second innings, the match was drawn and Carr had played his one and only Test Match. At the beginning of September, however, he bowled Lord Londesborough's XI to victory over the Australians at Scarborough.

For his performances during the season Carr was chosen as one of *Wisden*'s Five Cricketers of the Year and an appreciation appeared in the 1910 annual. Sydney H. Pardon wrote: 'During the season of 1908 one heard rumours that Kent possessed an excellent bowler of the South African ''googly'' type. I was told this myself and said to my informant, ''Why don't they let him loose without warning on Surrey or Yorkshire?'' ' Pardon's remarks underline the sense of mystery with which the leg-break and googly bowler was held and later he touches upon the misgivings that were felt in some quarters at their advent: 'Mr Carr is not one of those who think that ''googly'' bowling is going to rob batsmen of all their grace and freedom of style. On the contrary he says, ''I am quite certain of one thing, and that is that in a very short time everybody will be quite able to distinguish between the two breaks.'' '

Although he never played for England again, Carr maintained his form for Kent until the outbreak of the first world war and took 334 wickets in his six seasons. The leg-break and googly bowler throughout Carr's brief and late career remained something of an amateur eccentricity, but Carr had shown Kent the enormous value of such a bowler. It could have been one of the factors which prompted them to sign Alfred Percy Freeman as a member of their staff in 1912.

2
Debut,
1888–1918

'Tich' Freeman was born in Lewisham on 17 May 1888 into a cricketing family. His uncle, Edward Charles, had also been born in Lewisham, but had found his cricketing fortunes with Essex for whom he first played in 1887, seven years before the county had attained first-class status. He is chiefly remembered as a grounds-man rather than as a player, though, and it was he who was responsible for bringing the Leyton wicket up to first-class standard. One of his attempts at improvement went very much astray, however, when he asked Sam Apted, the Surrey curator, how he maintained such an excellent standard at The Oval with a view to doing the same at Leyton. Apted told him to apply a liquid mixture 'three days before the match'. Surrey were the next visitors to Leyton and when Essex won the toss they had no hesitation in batting on what they believed would be a perfect wicket. It turned out to be a sticky wicket of the most vicious kind and Essex were bowled out for 37 by Lockwood and Brockwell. One of the most attractive of fixtures between two good batting sides ended early on the second afternoon.

Freeman had misunderstood Apted's advice and had applied the liquid mixture on each of the three days before the game instead of only on the third day before the start of the match. He did not make the same mistake again and thereafter the Leyton wicket had a fine reputation. Edward Charles Freeman later became coach and groundsman at Sherborne School where he was succeeded by one of his six sons, Edward John.

Edward John Freeman played for Essex from 1904 to 1910 although he played only five championship matches in his last two seasons. He was a batsman and a wicket-keeper who never realised the hopes and expectations that were held of him. Indeed, in his seven seasons as an Essex player he scored only 1280 runs and, of those, 564 were made in 1907 when he hit a career-best 84 against Nottinghamshire at Trent Bridge. He followed his father to Sherborne and played for Dorset but, sadly, with little more success than he had enjoyed for Essex. He was a footballer of considerable ability and played 27 times for Essex. This was a passion he shared with his cousin, Alfred Percy, who also appeared for Essex at county level and assisted Leyton, Peterborough and Tunbridge Wells Rangers.

'Tich' had been on the ground staff at Leyton when his uncle was groundsman and played for Essex Club and Ground but, presumably, with insufficient success, for Essex did not engage him. They did engage his brother, John Robert, however, and he made his first class debut in 1905. He was a wicket-keeper batsman who gave Essex splendid service for over 20 years. He scored well over 14,000 runs for Essex, including 286 against Northamptonshire in 1921. Even in his last full season, 1926, he scored 1804 runs at an average of 39.21. He retired at the end of that season, when he was 43, to become coach at Merchant Taylors' School.

The batting performances of J. R. Freeman are significant because, in the opinion of those who played with him, 'Tich' Freeman could have been his brother's equal with the bat had he not given his life to bowling. He was to hit fifty on his Test debut and Howard Levett tells the story of a typical piece of Freeman batting determination at Folkestone in 1936, his last season with Kent. The match was against Glamorgan and Percy Chapman, the Kent captain, was becoming very impatient with Les Todd who was not hitting the ball with his usual vigour. It took Todd two and a half hours to complete fifty and Levett was sent in at no. 7 with a message to Todd from the skipper 'Get a hundred or you are dropped for the next match'.

Todd's chances of reaching a hundred depended almost entirely upon whether or not anyone would be able to stay with him. Levett's stay was very brief and although Chapman, Watt and Lewis all made a few runs, Todd was only 69 when Freeman joined him for the last wicket. Applying himself with that quiet enthusiasm which had pervaded his entire career, 'Tich' kept up his end and Todd was able to add 44 to his score before falling to Smart.

However, Kent had little interest in Freeman as a batsman when they asked him to join the staff at Tonbridge in 1912. From 1909 to 1911 he had played for Upper Tooting with some success and as a leg-break and googly bowler he was one of those mystery men whom R. E. Foster had seen as a threat to the aesthetic of batmanship.

Bosanquet's philosophy had been quite simple: 'The whole art of bowling is to make the batsman think that the ball is going to be of one kind when it is really of quite a different nature.' Following the visit of the South Africans, however, Foster had seen dark threats to the game if googly bowling took a hold. He wrote sombrely: 'I think it will cause a deterioration in batting. It must be realised that this type of bowling is practically in its infancy, and if persevered with – as it surely will be – must improve and become very difficult to deal with. Now a batsman when he goes in may receive a ball which either breaks from the off, perhaps from leg, or, again, may come straight through very quickly. If he survives half a dozen overs he ought to be getting set, but such bowling never allows a batsman to get really set, because he can never make or go for his accustomed shots. The ball just short of a half-volley, which he is accustomed to drive between cover and extra cover, now bothers him, and prevents him from doing so, owing to his inability to discover which way and how much the ball is going to break. And as this bowling improves, the difficulty will become increased, till those beautiful drives we are wont to expect from great batsmen will become a thing of the past.'

That 'this type of bowling is practically in its infancy' was undeniable in 1907, but by the time Freeman joined the Kent staff, Fender, 'Young Jack' Hearne, Grimmett and Mailey had all started their first-class careers, and it has already been noted that D. W. Carr's success may have had no small influence on Kent's decision to engage Freeman at the age of 24; although the little man's entry into first-class cricket was to be attended by none of the spectacular success which accompanied Carr's debut, the beginning of Freeman's career was to mark the end of Carr's.

Freeman's engagement by Kent was reported in splendidly anonymous fashion by the Young Players' Committee chairman, Captain McCanlis. In the report which followed the end of the 1911 season, a report which is only five lines long, it states: 'The services of Galley and Roberts have been dispensed with, and two other young men have been engaged for 1912.' Only a study of the batting and bowling averages of the young players in the following season reveals that the 'two other young men' were Freeman and Dutnall, F.

In 1912 Kent won more matches than any other county but finished only third in the Championship. The Committee's report for that season emphasises the county's desperate need for a fast bowler, even though all was well in the spin department with Carr, Blythe and Woolley, now a Test player, capturing nearly 350 wickets between them. Freeman had a very successful first season on the staff and in all 'young player' matches took 94 wickets at 10.57 runs apiece. These figures placed him third in the young players' bowling averages. His batting average was 12.24 and he is credited with a score of 80.

He was not in the Kent side for the opening second-team game of the season at The Oval and made his debut for Kent Club and Ground against White House, Catford, on 11 June. Kent Club and Ground won by an innings and 37 runs, White House being bowled out for 78 and 71. Freeman took the wickets of Mr H. A. Hooker and Mr W. S. Watts in a spell of ten overs in the first

15

innings in which he conceded 20 runs. The bowling honours went to Morfee who took 6 for 9 in 3.4 overs in the first innings, and to Draper who took 7 for 24 in the second innings in which Freeman did not bowl.

There was more serious stuff ahead and on 3 and 4 July 'Tich' Freeman played his first game for Kent 2nd XI against Staffordshire at West Malling. It was not a happy debut. Kent lost by nine wickets and Freeman did not bowl a ball in the entire match. It was an historic one, however, for opposed to the man who was to become the greatest wicket-taker in county cricket was a man who was to be considered by many to be the greatest of bowlers, S. F. Barnes. 'Tich', batting at no. 11, was bowled Barnes 5 and caught and bowled Barnes 1. Barnes took 12 for 85 in the match and the young Kent bowler making his debut looked on and no doubt pondered about line and length.

In spite of taking 6 for 9 for the Club and Ground against Gore Court at Sittingbourne, holding two catches and taking another three wickets in the second innings, Freeman did not play in the return game with Staffordshire. He did travel down to Truro and on 22 and 23 July played a part in Kent's victory over Cornwall. In the first innings he bowled two overs and took 2 for 0 (nos. 10 and 11) and in the second innings he bowled three overs and took 1 for 1. Coupled with his success in other games, it was enough to help him maintain his 2nd XI place for the rest of the season.

He took 4 for 13 and 3 for 31 against Dorset at Poole and one wicket in the rain-restricted return game at Beckenham. When Cornwall came to Gravesend for the return game he took five wickets in each innings, six of them clean bowled, and conceded only 52 runs. It was his last success of the season in a senior game for he bowled little for the Club and Ground in their two remaining fixtures (XVI of Ashford and District mustered only 79 against Preston and Smith), and against Surrey 2nd XI at Hythe he failed to take a wicket.

His last game of the season for the Club and Ground is of interest for the Kent side were beaten by four wickets by the Band of Brothers who included in their side Lord Harris, Nigel Haig and

D. W. Carr. Freeman met with no success in his six overs, but Carr twice routed his own county, taking 4 for 31 and 5 for 31. Of course, he opened the bowling.

It had been a satisfactory first season for the new leg-break and googly bowler. His 21 wickets in 2nd XI matches had cost him only 168 runs and his average of 8.00 placed him second to Preston in the bowling averages, but there was better to come in 1913.

In 1913, Kent won the County Championship for the fourth time in eight years. They won 20 of their 28 matches and lost only three. They were not to win the Championship for another 57 years, but only in retrospect does one see the end of an era. Blythe, Woolley, Fielder and Carr (in August) all bowled splendidly and, in his forty-third year, Fred Huish beat his own wicket-keeping record of 100 dismissals set up in 1911 by helping to send back 102 batsmen, 32 of them stumped – the shape of things to come.

As *Wisden* pointed out in their summary of the season, 'No new talent was discovered, the players being almost identical with those in 1912.' The new talent was, in fact, performing nobly in the 2nd XI. In his opening remarks at the beginning of the report of the Young Players' Committee, the chairman, Kenneth McAlpine, stated: 'Mr Weigall reports that he considers great progress was made by some of the Young Players, particularly Freeman and Dutnall. Freeman promising well as a googly bowler, and Dutnall showing great advancement as a bat.'

In the young players' averages Freeman was credited with 125 wickets during the season at a cost of 12.69 runs each. He was easily the leading wicket-taker. He was also leading wicket-taker in the Club and Ground matches and, most importantly, was top of the 2nd XI bowling averages with 44 wickets at 13.72 each. He had three more wickets than Preston, second in the averages, who left the staff at the end of the season. As *Wisden* noted, 'Freeman and Preston bowled with distinct success. Beyond these two, however, there were no bowlers of note.' This was a statement with more than a hint of prophecy in it for over much of the next

24 years Freeman was to carry the Kent bowling almost entirely upon his own shoulders.

He was quickly into his stride in 1913, taking four wickets in the opening 2nd XI match at The Oval. In the return game at Tonbridge he spun Surrey to defeat with 5 for 36 in the second innings. He opened the bowling, for the fetish of speed was not yet with us.

His greatest triumph was to come in the next match, the drawn game with Staffordshire at Canterbury on 14 and 15 July. On the opening morning, coming on after six overs had been bowled, he immediately had Briggs stumped and then took the next eight wickets as Staffordshire slipped from 25 for 0 to 106 for 9. Unfortunately Preston robbed him of all ten wickets when he bowled Scott. Freeman's final figures were 13−1−36−9. Kent attained a lead of 67 and the match was drawn with Staffordshire 91 for 5 in their second innings, Freeman 4 for 38. Kent were soundly beaten in the return game at Stoke where Barnes returned to the Staffordshire side to take 6 for 39 in the second innings. Freeman had 4 for 90 and clean bowled Barnes, never a mean feat.

There were ten wickets against Glamorgan, not yet a first-class county, and a thoroughly satisfactory season was concluded, but Freeman was already 25 years old and he had still not played first-class cricket.

As a 'Young Player' Freeman took 135 wickets in Kent representative matches in 1914, but far overshadowing his performances in minor cricket was the fact that he made his first-class debut: he was given a place in the Kent side that played Oxford University in The Parks on 25, 26 and 27 May.

Oxford University batted first on what, inevitably, was a good wicket, and Fairservice and Woolley opened the bowling, but it was not until Colin Blythe came into the attack that wickets fell. Humphreys was the next to bowl and then, third change, came Freeman. There was none of the immediate and romantic success that Carr had enjoyed five years previously almost to the day on the same ground. P. H. S. Davies and C. R. S. Rucker added 83 for the varsity's last wicket before Davies, having hit 55 at no. 10, jumped out to Freeman and was stumped by Fred Huish. It was the first of 484 stumpings taken off him during his career. He had bowled 18.2 overs and his one wicket had cost him 88 runs. There had been one maiden over.

When Kent batted in response to Oxford's 337, runs came freely; James Seymour hit 122, Mr Troughton hit 104, the only century of his career, Captain Sarel hit 93, a career-best, and Frank Woolley made 75. Kent reached 571. Freeman was bowled by Bristowe for nought, the only player, along with Humphreys, not to reach double figures. Oxford made 323 for 5 in their second innings and Freeman dismissed Howell and Wilkinson, both lbw, for 109 runs conceded in 20 overs. He returned to the 2nd XI.

Moderate success against Monmouthshire was followed by a splendid performance against Surrey 2nd XI at The Oval on the first two days of July. Four for 81 in the first innings was followed by 5 for 107 in the second and he numbered Sandham, Peach and 'Razor' Smith among his victims. Four days later he took 11 wickets in the match against Lincolnshire, which Kent lost, and then, at the end of July, he took 5 for 57 and 5 for 6 in Kent's victory over Staffordshire (and Barnes) at Gravesend. There were seven wickets against Lincolnshire at Woodhall Spa and eight against Essex 2nd XI at Leyton, both games being won, and then 7 for 55 against Staffordshire at Stoke in a game which Kent lost by an innings, Barnes taking 10 for 25 and Freeman bagging a 'pair'. This was, in fact, Freeman's last game for the 2nd XI for there had been an important event in the first team.

On 30 July Surrey visited Blackheath for their annual encounter with Kent, in Kent, a fixture which they had not won for 17 years. Kent were running second in the championship with Middlesex, Surrey being the leaders. The home county had Douglas Carr available for the first time in the season and Kentish hopes were high. Their hopes soared higher as they made 349 on the Thursday, even though they could not separate Hobbs and Hayward before the close. On the Friday Hobbs and Hayward took their opening stand to 234, both hitting 122, and then D. J. Knight scored 105 and Surrey totalled 509. In the end the match was drawn and Surrey went on to win the title.

During the course of the Surrey innings Carr appeared to have lost all control over length, line and the ability to turn the ball. He bowled 28 overs and conceded 134 runs without taking a wicket. He received a terrible hammering from Hobbs and Hayward and was so depressed that he asked not to be included in the county side for the remainder of the season. It was a fateful request.

On the Friday, while Carr had been receiving his battering at the hands of the Surrey batsmen, the British Foreign Secretary had been asking Germany for an assurance that she would respect the neutrality of Belgium. By the August Bank Holiday Monday, when Kent were at Canterbury playing Sussex without Carr, Germany had declared war on Russia and her troops were massing on the Belgian border. On Monday 3 August 1914, Germany invaded Belgium and Great Britain declared war. Not only was the first-class career of D. W. Carr at an end, so was the world that the cricketers of the Golden Age had known.

At the outbreak of war some counties cancelled at least some of their remaining fixtures. Kent did not, and the Committee defended its decision in their annual report: 'The Committee have been subjected to some criticism over their decision to complete the programme of the Season: in doing so the Committee were solely guided by the desire to comply with the wishes of Government not to add to the number of unemployed by cancelling their arrangements and as far as it lay in their powers to hold to normal conditions. Some of their critics were perhaps forgetful of the fact that during the greater part of August there was no recruiting allowed for the Territorial Army and that the maximum age was 30, which disqualified a large proportion of the Kent County players.'

Things did not continue as normal, however, The Army requisitioned The Oval and arrangements were made hurriedly to transfer two of Surrey's matches to Lord's where the annual schools' fixtures had been cancelled. One of the matches to be affected was Jack Hobbs' benefit match, Surrey v. Kent. Hobbs was given the choice of taking his benefit at Lord's or postponing it until after the war; he elected to have it at Lord's.

The Kent team for the match showed one change from the side which had lost to Sussex and beaten Northants by an innings since the Blackheath encounter with Surrey: A. P. Freeman replaced W. J. Fairservice.

As a benefit it was a disaster for Jack Hobbs. Hitch took nine wickets in the match, Percy Fender five, and Kent were beaten in two days. The takings were poor and the restricted collection brought in much less than it would have done at The Oval. Surrey offered to discount it as a benefit, retaining the gate-money, keeping the subscription list open and re-staging the match after the war. Hobbs accepted their generous offer.

Kent were out for 140 in both innings, Freeman not out 1 and bowled Hitch 0. Fielder and Blythe opened the Kent bowling with Woolley coming on at first change and Freeman at second change. He bowled 11 quite tidy overs for 42 runs but did not take a wicket. Indeed, nine of the Surrey wickets were taken by 'Charlie' Blythe at a cost of 97 runs. It was the last great performance of a noble and elegant cricketer. As a sergeant in the King's Own Yorkshire Light Infantry, he was killed at Ypres in November 1917. His final flourish on the cricket field was made in the game in which the man who was to succeed him as Kent's leading bowler was making his County Championship debut.

Surrey needed only 47 to win and Freeman opened the second innings bowling with Fielder. With the score at 9 he deceived Tom Hayward with a cleverly flighted leg-break and bowled him, an impressive first County Championship wicket which cost him, eventually, 20 runs.

It was not a sensational debut but 'Tich' had shown a quality that caught the eye of some discerning judges. Sydney H. Pardon, editor of *Wisden*, remarked nine years later how fine an achievement it had seemed at the time that such an inexperienced bowler could so trouble the great Tom Hayward.

From Lord's Kent travelled to Birmingham where they beat Warwickshire in a match dominated by the bowlers and in which Freeman took five wickets in an innings for the first time in his career; he was to accomplish the feat on another 385 occasions in the next 22 years. Warwickshire batted first and Kinneir and Smith seemed in little trouble against Fielder, Blythe and Woolley, but Freeman bowled both openers and then had F. R. Foster caught by Seymour, bowled Baker, Jeeves and Field, and caught and bowled Santall. (Jeeves, of course, was the Warwickshire all-rounder, killed in action in 1916, whose name was used by the great cricket-lover, P. G. Wodehouse, for the immortal character that he created.) In ten overs Freeman had taken 7 for 25 and Warwickshire were out for 111. Kent could only equal this score, but Warwickshire managed just 78 in their second innings, Fielder taking 7 for 34, Blythe 2 for 4 and Freeman 1 for 29. Kent won by nine wickets.

Freeman played in all the remaining matches and took a wicket every time he bowled. He had 3 for 42 in the first innings of the return match with Warwickshire at Gravesend – Jeeves, stumped Huish – and 8 for 129 in the match against Middlesex at Lord's. His victims included Nigel Haig in both innings and Patsy Hendren in the second innings, caught at slip by Woolley – caught Woolley, bowled Freeman was an entry which was to tire the scorers for the next two decades.

The season ended with something of a hammering at Bourne-mouth and, when first-class cricket was abandoned for nearly five years, Freeman had taken 29 wickets in the season at a cost of 27.55 runs each. Appendix F to *The History of Kent County Cricket* commented, 'Freeman, appearing for the team in eight matches, commenced his County career in modest fashion.' His 57 wickets for the 2nd XI had been secured at 12.47 runs each. He was clearly above second-team standard, but he was 26 years old and first-class cricket was in abeyance for the duration of the war.

Like many of his generation Alf Freeman found himself in limbo. He was a married man (of Ethel more will be said later) who knew no other life but cricket, nor did he ever conceive of any life that was not connected with the game in some way. As Howard Levett, Freeman's Kent team-mate, has said, 'You could never imagine Alf doing anything else. You could never think of him as being in an army, for example.' It is perhaps hard to imagine how many men whom we meet in later life passed their younger days, but Alf Freeman, like the rest of the 'seed of Europe' and the cricketers exhorted by W. G. Grace's cry, served. He did not fly instantly to the colours as Blythe had done, rather he fitted the description of Auden's 'Unknown Citizen': 'When there was peace, he was for peace; when there was war, he went.'

3
Reaching the Top, 1919–21

The war destroyed much and changed much. At the end of 1919 the Kent membership stood at little more than half of what it had been in 1914. Lord Harris and Mr Pawley, the Kent manager, met the leading professionals to discuss wages and expenses and inevitably, the Committee announced that subscriptions and entrance fees would have to be raised. Their plaintive cry has a familiar ring: ' . . . members will realise that they can not expect to get now – when the expense of carrying out the match Programme and re-organising the Club Cricket with a view to producing the best Eleven possible is double what it was pre-war – the Privileges of the Club at the same cost. The Committee propose in the first place to lay the burden on the public by raising the Entrance fee at Canterbury Week. Out of the extra sixpence charged last year only 2d came to the Club, the other 4d being taken for Entertainment Tax. The pre-War Entrance Fee was 1/-: as Expenses have about doubled the Committee feel themselves justified in raising the entrance fee to 2/-.' There was the problem, too, of financing the memorial to Colin Blythe and the other Kent players, notably Hutchings, who fell in the war. For the time being, at least, the concern over the cricket itself had to become almost secondary.

If there was an upheaval in the social and economic conditions

24

of the country, however, many traditions survived and Freeman was one who accepted social conventions unquestioningly. He had, after all, joined the county in 1912, the twilight of the Golden Age. In that year the Committee's gravest concern, reflecting the unwavering demand for standards, had been covered by the President in the final paragraph of his report: 'The Committee regret to state that two members of the Club were found to have accepted pass-out tickets at a County match last July, and to have made use of these for the admission of their friends later in the day. Both these members have been informed that subscriptions will not be accepted from them next year.'

It is important, when considering Freeman both as a cricketer and as a man, to remember that this was the climate when he first played for Kent and that this was the social discipline that he accepted all his life. He was neither a revolutionary, nor was he a moaner. Brian Valentine, one of his last captains, tells how the bitterest complaint that he ever heard the man make was when it was suggested that he should have a rest from bowling as there seemed little sign of a wicket falling. 'Give me a couple more, skipper,' he would plead. 'I'm sure that I can get him in a minute.'

From that first game at Oxford in 1914 until his last at Folkestone in 1936, he gave his very best, tried his very hardest with every ball and accepted the authority of those whom, rightly or wrongly, he considered his superiors. In this he reflected the outlook of the great majority of his contemporaries among cricket professionals. He was reared in the days when amateurs and professionals stayed in different hotels and changed in different dressing rooms, and when the senior professional's position among his fellows was one of unquestioned leadership, on and off the field. Alf Freeman would have readily understood J. T. Hearne's standing in the Middlesex team as described by Harry Lee: 'J. T. Hearne was in charge of us, and there was a set hour for us to be at meals or in bed. When we came to sit down, the juniors stood back until the seniors had chosen their places. Then J. T. would take his seat at the head of the table, and carve the joint, handing round the plates in proper order of seniority, and giving himself the carver's portion last of all.'

The most startling change imposed upon first-class cricket during the season immediately after the war was the restriction of matches to two days instead of three. Lord Harris was strongly opposed to the shortening of the duration of matches, so Kent arranged only 14 fixtures in 1919: Middlesex, Hampshire, Essex, Sussex, Lancashire, Yorkshire and Surrey were played on a home and away basis. The Australian Imperial Forces were entertained in a three-day game at Canterbury. Freeman played in each of these 15 games and finished the season with 55 wickets at 19.41 runs each, an average which placed him second only to Woolley who took 90 wickets in bowling exactly twice as many overs as the googly bowler.

Freeman's season began quietly. There were 5 for 4 for the Club and Ground as he and Howlett bowled out St Lawrence College, Ramsgate, for 22, but in the 1st XI it was Frank Woolley who was dominating the Kent bowling. Freeman had six wickets in the match against Hampshire at Tunbridge Wells in mid-July and one of his victims was Hon. Lionel Tennyson who hit a hundred in the second innings before falling lbw to 'Tich'. Mead and Brown were the other wickets, a formidable trio.

The dismissal of Tennyson was the first that Freeman had in a long line of victories over the colourful Hampshire skipper. Invariably Tennyson would leap out at 'Tich', miss and be stumped, or go back, be beaten by the googly and find himself lbw. Les Ames recalls one occasion when Tennyson won the toss on a perfect wicket at Canterbury and went back to the pavilion chuckling. He poked his head round the door of the Kent professionals' dressing room and bellowed, 'Where is the little bugger? It's a perfect wicket out there to-day. This is the day I'm going to have you.' When it was his turn to bat Lord Tennyson came to the wicket with a gleam in his eye and shouted down the wicket, 'Watch out, Tich, I'm going to hit you clean out of the ground.'

His boast caused roars of laughter in the Kent side, but next over he hit a magnificent shot through the covers and then straight-drove a splendid six into the pavilion. He could not conceal his glee. Two balls later 'Tich' tossed up seemingly the same ball and Tennyson jumped out to hit him again, but it was tossed a little higher and was just a little wider and with just the right amount of turn. The Hampshire captain drove, missed – stumped Ames, bowled Freeman. He strode angrily from the field cursing himself. At the close of play he came to the Kent professionals' dressing room again and said, 'It's no use, "Tich", you've got the better of me. If I go forward I'm stumped; if I go back I'm lbw. I shall never know how to play you.'

Following the game with Hampshire came Kent's greatest triumph of the season when they beat the old enemy, Surrey, by 136 runs at Blackheath. Hardinge played a superb innings of 97 out of 164 and then Woolley and Fairservice bowled the visitors out for 75. Seymour hit a hundred and Surrey needed 340 to win. Woolley, who had done the hat-trick in the first innings, sent back Knight, Ducat and Howell, but Hobbs was at his most majestic and hit a brilliant hundred. Then came Freeman. He took the last four wickets in six balls (three of them in four balls), finished with 6 for 43, and Surrey were beaten.

His first taste of Australian opposition came in the game against the AIF at the beginning of August. It was a high-scoring game which ended in a draw. Freeman dismissed Pellew twice in the match and had figures of 3 for 41 and 2 for 100. He then had two splendid matches, at Bournemouth against Hampshire and at Brighton against Sussex. Hampshire were beaten by an innings and 'Tich' took 7 for 71 and 6 for 56 – Tennyson fell to him twice. This represented his best haul to date in first-class cricket and his bowling was causing favourable comment. He took six of the last seven wickets as Sussex crashed from 54 for 3 to 100 all out at Brighton and he had 10 for 124 in the match.

At The Oval, Kent suffered their only defeat of the season. This was Jack Hobbs' benefit match, five years later than originally scheduled. Surrey were left 42 minutes in which to make 95 runs to win. J. N. Crawford and Jack Hobbs hit the runs required in 32 minutes, scoring at eight an over. There seemed no suggestion of Kent asking to leave the field even though the match finished in pouring rain.

Moving to their last match of the season at Lord's, Kent needed to win to gain the Championship. They came tantalisingly close. 109 behind on the first innings, Middlesex passed fifty without loss in the second innings and then began to crumble. Freeman sent back 'Plum' Warner, G. T. S. Stevens and Gunasekara, but at the close of play Middlesex were 121 for 9, just twelve runs ahead, the match was a draw and Kent were second to Yorkshire in the County Championship. It was the highest position that they were to attain in Freeman's career. In all matches he had taken 60 wickets and, according to *The History of Kent County Cricket*, 'by a series of useful performances, made his place in the side secure and more than once . . . foreshadowed his future greatness.'

During that first season after the war three cricketers whose careers were to be connected with Freeman's in one way or another made their debuts in first-class cricket. Two leg-break and googly bowlers, Richard Tyldesley and C. S. Marriott, appeared for Lancashire. Tyldesley was a Falstaffian figure whose career was to be shorter and far less productive than Freeman's, but who was to be preferred to the Kent man in home Test matches against Australia. Marriott had been born in Lancashire and brought up in Ireland. When he played for Lancashire against Essex at Leyton in May 1919, it was the first time that he had ever been present at a county game. Later, of course, he was to play for Kent after his years at Cambridge.

The third of the trio was an 18-year-old schoolboy at University College School, Greville Thomas Scott Stevens. Stevens was an 'infant' prodigy; he had scored 466 in a house match while at preparatory school. (It would be interesting to explore the identities of the unfortunate children who had to bowl to Stevens during this innings and those who had to bowl to A. E. J. Collins for five afternoons while he made 628 not out for Clark's House against North Town at Clifton College in 1899; it might even be more rewarding to explore the motives of the schoolmasters who allowed these innings to go on as long as they did.) Stevens was selected to play for the Gentlemen against the Players at Lord's in 1919 – shades of D. W. Carr – and scored 24 and 11. He had

Kennedy of Hampshire lbw in the first innings and conceded 62
runs in the match. Later in the season he played for Middlesex and
again for the Gentlemen at Scarborough.

One mentions Stevens because it is interesting to compare his
Test record with Freeman's:

	Tests	Runs	Wickets	Catches
		Average	*Average*	
Freeman	12	154	66	4
		14.00	25.86	
Stevens	10	263	20	9
		15.47	32.40	

Yet Stevens was always seen as the golden boy. One possible
reason may be difficult to appreciate now, some twenty years after
'gentlemen' and 'players' became just 'cricketers', but Stevens –
like Robins and Peebles after him – was in that tradition of amateur
leg-break and googly bowlers who later were seen as likely to be
more effective than the durable professional. Back in 1898, Hon.
R. H. Lyttleton had written in *The Badminton Book of Cricket*:
'We would not say one word against the personal character of the
English professional cricketer, for the great majority of this class
are honest, hard-working and sober men. We only say that it is not
in the interests of cricket that any branch of the game should be left
entirely in their hands.' Even 32 years later J. C. Squire could still
write: 'It stands to reason that cricket dominated by amateurs
must be livelier than cricket in which professionals (though there
are many exceptions among these) set the tone.'

It was this emphasis on liveliness that dominated the thinking
that the amateur leg-break bowler (who, as Squire says later, must
be enjoying himself, thereby implying that the professional was
not) would be much more likely to produce the unpredictable and
unplayable. He could afford to experiment, to gamble; the professional could not. The amateur had a romantic dash about him; the
professional had not. Such was the accepted thinking of the time
among followers of the game and among the selectors – themselves amateurs.

G. T. S. Stevens was part of the Middlesex side that won the
Championship in 1920, Sir Pelham Warner's last season. It was a

29

fascinating domestic season with matches reverting to three days duration and the stimulation of the resumption of Test cricket at the end of the season when an MCC side would go to Australia. Still without a pace bowler, Kent, helped by many slow wickets, did remarkably well. They began by winning their first four matches (Freeman taking 5 for 40 in the Warwickshire second innings of the opening match) and although they lost twice to Lancashire and once to Sussex, they reached August still in contention for the title having won six more matches. 'Tich' took 5 for 14 against Leicestershire in their first innings at Tunbridge Wells, but otherwise his performances were steady rather than spectacular.

In the first week in August Kent met Middlesex at Canterbury. It was a wonderful game that had much to do with the ultimate destiny of the Championship. Harry Lee and H. L. Dales opened against the bowling of Fairservice and Woolley, who was having a marvellous all-round season. The great left-arm bowler dismissed Lee and then Freeman joined the attack to send back Dales, 'Plum' Warner and F. T. Mann, the first and third lbw, the second bowled. His figures were 3 for 55 in 14 overs. Woolley had four wickets and Middlesex were out for 212. Thanks to a second-wicket stand of 139 between Hardinge and Seymour, Kent gained a first-innings lead of five runs.

When Middlesex batted again Woolley sent back both openers with 23 on the board. Again Freeman was first change. With the score on 47 he had J. W. Hearne, 'Young Jack', lbw; next ball F. T. Mann edged a leg-break to Seymour at slip, then Nigel Haig was bowled first ball to give 'Tich' the first hat-trick of his career. He later bowled Hendren, Murrell and Durston to finish with 6 for 36 in 11.3 overs. Later detractors were to argue that Alf Freeman only captured the 'rabbits', but such an assertion is nonsense and few cricketers can claim a hat-trick comprising three such august victims as Freeman's first.

There was no happy ending, however, for Kent, needing 123 to win and 70 for 1 at one time, were all out for 117. 'Young Jack' Hearne took 8 for 26 (he had been hammered in the first innings) and Middlesex moved on to their memorable Championship win.

Throughout August Freeman bowled with success. He bowled with such turn and control in the second innings of the match at The Oval that he once more excited favourable comment from Sydney H. Pardon. Surrey had been set 290 to win, not an easy task, but it seemed simple after Hobbs and Sandham had put on 192 for the first wicket. Freeman then bowled Sandham, Knight and Peach, and Surrey just got home by three wickets. *Wisden* reported, 'Freeman, who kept a marvellous length with his leg-breaks and googlies, paralysed the later batsmen, and in the end Surrey scrambled home ingloriously.' This opinion was reiterated in the review that preceded the Kent match section where the unequivocal statement was made that Freeman 'has a better command over his pitch than any other googly bowler in the country'.

'Tich' took eight wickets at Lord's in the penultimate match of the county season, so bringing his total to 98. In the last match of the season at Trent Bridge Nottinghamshire batted first on a beautiful wicket and Whysall and Gunn opened with a century stand. Frank Woolley sent back Whysall and John Gunn at 122. At 150, A. W. Carr was stumped by Hubble off Freeman and then George Gunn, having hit his second century of the season, was caught by Hardinge to give Freeman 100 wickets in a season for the first time in his career. He claimed Joe Hardstaff senior and G. M. Lee for good measure and that day sent down more than 50 overs in an innings for the first time. In view of what was to come both feats now seem trivial, but Freeman had passed into the front rank of English spinners.

He was to play one more first-class match that season, his first taste of representative cricket, when he appeared for the South versus the North at Hastings in the first week in September. He bowled 21 overs in the match and did not take a wicket, although he did score 25 in a brisk last-wicket partnership with A. E. R. Gilligan.

It is impossible to say whether the selectors ever considered sending Freeman to Australia for the 1920–21 series. As

England were beaten by five Tests to nil he was probably well out of it. Cecil Parkin considered that the side that J. W. H. T. Douglas led to Australia that winter was one of the strongest that ever sailed from Tilbury. Hobbs, Hendren, Woolley, Fender, Rhodes, Strudwick, Parkin himself – the names tend to support that view, but there was a strong similarity between the fate that awaited Douglas' team and the fate that awaited Hammond's after the second world war. In truth, the difference between England and Australia on both occasions lay mainly in the difference in the cricketing health of the two nations after the ravages of war.

Parkin had spent most of the 1920 season playing league cricket for Rochdale, but had made enough appearances for Lancashire to win him a place in the 16. Ultimately, Parkin was to concentrate upon off-breaks, bowled round the wicket to a leg trap, but in the seasons just after the first war he bowled virtually everything, including the leg-break and googly. There were two more specialised leg-break and googly bowlers in the 16, however – Percy Fender and J. W. Hearne, the latter selected only at the eleventh hour.

Fender finished top of the England bowling averages in the Tests, taking 12 wickets in the 100 overs he bowled, but it was a leg-break and googly bowler on the other side who stole all the headlines. His name was Arthur Mailey. During the series Mailey took 36 wickets at 26.27 runs each, including 9 for 121 in the second innings of the fourth Test. This total of 36 wickets in a series remained an Australian record for 58 years. It was achieved at the beginning of an era of wickets which were to produce 500 runs in a second innings on several occasions and which were twice to produce 1,000 runs in an innings, once with Mailey bowling. Mailey, a witty and charming man, imparted a great deal of spin on the ball which he tossed high into the air, but his length and general accuracy, even variety, could not compare with Freeman's.

Australia were captained by Warwick Armstrong who also bowled leg-breaks with considerable success and took nine wickets in the 1920–21 series. Before sailing for England for the 1921 season Armstrong prophesied that Australia would defeat England as easily in England as they had done in Australia. He was right.

The Australian touring side of 1921 is one of the legendary sides. McDonald and Gregory spearheaded the attack and Mailey and Armstrong removed any other irritations. It was a highly successful combination, but the Australian captain won few friends. As Kenneth Gregory expressed it so beautifully, 'Armstrong's circus provided rare entertainment, its ringmaster provoked much abuse.'

In the match against Kent at Canterbury on 10, 11 and 12 August, before a huge crowd, Armstrong batted on until the second afternoon as his side amassed 676 (Freeman had 0 for 138) and then refused to enforce the follow-on when Kent were bowled out for 237. Australia indulged in the second innings in meaningless batting practice (Freeman bowled McDonald) so that they would not be tired for the fifth Test match which started the next day. And they were already 3–0 up in the series! The Australians' attitude evoked unfavourable comment from Lord Harris in the annual report to Kent members: 'The Committee take this their only opportunity of offering to the spectators during the Australian match at Canterbury their appreciation of the dignified attitude maintained, notwithstanding the irritation they must have suffered at the extraordinary tactics adopted by Mr Armstrong.'

Even more bewildering in that hot, dry summer of 1921 was the fact that although the selectors chose no less than 30 players to represent England in the five Tests that year, Alfred Percy Freeman was not one of them. Fender, J. W. Hearne, who had not bowled well in Australia and who was injured for much of 1921, and Richmond of Notts all played in the Tests, but not Freeman whose record was far superior to any of them. He began the season with five second-innings wickets for Kent against MCC which gave Kent victory by 30 runs. He dismissed R. H. Spooner twice in the match and from that day went from success to success. Six times that season he took ten wickets in a match for Kent, 14 times five wickets in an innings. It was the first of the great years.

At Northampton, at the end of May, he took 8 for 22, then a career-best, in the first innings. Later in the year he took 8 for 78 against Worcestershire. For the first time he dismissed brother Jack, bowling him twice at Leyton and then again at Tunbridge Wells. While he was taking his 13 wickets for 67 at Northampton England were losing to Australia in two days at Trent Bridge. In this first Test match the England spin attack was in the hands of Woolley, Rhodes, V. W. C. Jupp and Richmond. Thomas Leonard Richmond was a 31-year-old, portly leg-break and googly bowler. He was a notoriously poor fielder and a meagre batsman. In what was to be his only Test match he bowled well enough to take the wickets of Collins and Gregory and to excite the comment, 'Richmond's googlies having to be very carefully watched'. Yet *Wisden*, not usually given to comparisons, later said of Freeman: 'By common consent he bowled better googlies than anyone else in county cricket, being in this respect decidedly superior to Richmond of Notts.'

It was not the last time that Test selectors were to disappoint Alf Freeman, although in his entire career he was never to reveal the slightest trace of any sadness he may have felt at the treatment he received. He accepted all triumphs and disasters equally; they were simply part of the job of being a professional cricketer.

In August, at Hastings, he performed a feat which for two years was to remain his career-best. Even this feat must have been tinged with some regret. Woolley was playing for England at The Oval and Sussex led Kent by 110 runs on the first innings. When Sussex batted again Freeman had Jupp lbw with the score at 40 and had captured three more wickets before the score had reached a hundred. As he had not come on until second change, this is one of those matches that tends to refute the argument that he took wickets only after he had conceded quite a few runs. He continued to take wickets until he had 9 for 87 at which point Gilligan declared, so denying him all ten. He was to be revenged on Sussex for that.

At the end of June he was in the Players' team against the Gentlemen at The Oval for the first time. He dismissed Captain

Jameson in both innings and E. L. Kidd in the second. The Players won by an innings with just over a quarter of an hour to spare. It was a close thing, for the finish was scheduled for 4.30 so that many from both sides could travel to Leeds in time to play in the third Test which began the following day. It was Hearne and Freeman who finished off the Gentlemen's second innings and gave the Players their victory against the clock, but it was Jack Durston whose bowling made the victory possible. Bowling as quickly and as well as he had ever done, Durston produced a spell in which he bowled Jeacocke, Morrison, Crawford and Haig at a personal cost of 21 runs. It was superb bowling and he was somewhat surprised to be called from the field shortly after taking his fourth wicket. He was told that the selection committee had been so impressed by his bowling that he was to go home and prepare himself for the journey to Leeds where he was to join the England team for the third Test which began the following morning. He did as he was asked, but when the England players took the field at Leeds he was not among them. In fact, Durston, who had made his international debut in the second Test, never played Test cricket again, so Freeman was not alone in having cause to muse upon the vagaries of selectors. 1921 was not the most memorable of seasons for English cricket, on or off the field.

A week after the Gentlemen v. Players match Mr G. G. F. Greig, the Worcestershire no. 11, pushed forward at a leg-break pitched on middle and off and was caught at slip by Frank Woolley. It was Freeman's hundredth wicket of the season and he was the first bowler in the country to reach that mark. He finished the season on 166 wickets, only Woolley (167) and the Hampshire pair, Newman and Kennedy, taking more.

In 1921, Freeman used the googly to great effect, but it would be wrong to suppose that all leg-break bowlers use, or even have command of, the googly. C. S. Marriott, who in 1921 took 66 wickets, most of them for Cambridge University, stated that he did not bowl the googly in first-class cricket until some years after he had begun to play for Kent, and then only because he had been cajoled and persuaded by 'Tich' Freeman. Freeman himself used the googly less as years went on, but by the end of 1921 he was one of the world's leading exponents whose true worth remained to some extent, and certainly in terms of international cricket, still unrecognised.

The England disasters of 1921 are often thought now to have been the exclusive work of Gregory and McDonald, but this was not the case. In the ravages that were caused throughout the country Arthur Mailey's leg-breaks and googlies had a striking rate comparable to the lightning deliveries of Gregory and McDonald, and in that memorable match at Eastbourne at the end of August when A. C. MacLaren's England XI became the first side to defeat the Australians, another leg-break and googly bowler, Aubrey Faulkner, played a leading role, taking 4 for 50 and 2 for 13 as well as scoring 3 and 153.

Perhaps Aubrey Faulkner's all-round performance highlights what England selectors seemed to want of their leg-break bowlers. In Fender (whose bowling, like that of Parkin and S. F. Barnes, was of such variety that it really defies a category), J. W. Hearne and G. T. S. Stevens, they had men who could both bat and bowl, and often such cricketers are preferred to those who have a speciality in one field or the other. Even Richie Benaud, the greatest leg-break bowler to emerge since the second world war, asserts that he only got into the Australian side because he was a leg-break bowler who could bat, and that he would not have been selected as a bowler alone.

4
MCC Tourist, 1922–23

The successes that Alfred Freeman had had in 1921 paled into insignificance beside his achievements of the following season. He and Frank Woolley together took 336 wickets; the other bowlers in the Kent side took only 145. As Frank Thorogood of the *Daily News* said, '"The Long and the Short of Kent" made a formidable pair', and yet, although he took 142 wickets in the season for Kent, 1922 saw the first signs of Frank Woolley's decline as a bowler. With a bat in his hand, he was to remain the loveliest sight on a cricket field for the next 16 years, but his ability to spin the ball, especially on a good wicket, began to diminish and more and more work was to pass onto the shoulders of 'Tich' Freeman. Although George Collins took 16 wickets against Nottinghamshire at Dover, including all ten in the second innings, and finished the season with 75 wickets for 18.62 runs each, the lack of support bowling for Freeman was already evident. As *The History of Kent County Cricket*, Appendix F, somewhat apologetically said of Collins: '. . . it is doing him no injustice to say that, apart from his great triumph against Nottinghamshire at Dover, he was quite an ordinary bowler.'

Freeman was far from being an ordinary bowler. He was, said *Wisden*, 'at the top of his form, keeping a remarkable length

37

to his leg-breaks, and every now and then bowling genuine and well-disguised googlies. Seldom or never did he fail to take advantage of a treacherous wicket.' He bowled in 51 innings that year and failed to take a wicket on only four occasions. Only in the game with the champions, Yorkshire, at Leeds, when he bowled only 11 overs, did he not take a wicket in a match. Like good wine, his season grew better as it grew older. It ended as the richest of vintages.

In the third match of the season he took six Worcestershire first-innings wickets for 36 runs at Gravesend to put Kent on the way to an innings victory. This performance was in no respect remarkable by Freeman's standards (after all, he took six wickets in an innings on 129 occasions), but there was one incident worthy of note. The Worcestershire batsman, W. H. Taylor, hit a delivery from Freeman over the pavilion at Gravesend, an achievement which rightly earned him immortality in the record books. What the record books so rarely mention is the sequel:

Taylor c Solbe, b Freeman   6

Few batsmen ever trifled with 'Tich' Freeman more than once.

Six and seven wickets in an innings became almost commonplace for 'Tich' in 1922, but there were some performances which must have given him particular pleasure. For most supporters the Kent v. Surrey games were the highlights of the season, and Kent's ten-wicket victory at Blackheath, a ground which held few happy memories for Surrey, elated Kentish men. A huge crowd watched play on the first day, although there were several stoppages for rain which ended the match an hour early. Woolley had played a magnificent innings of 75 and Kent reached 243 on the Monday after rain had delayed the start. In just over an hour and a half Surrey were bowled out for 77. Coming on after four overs had been bowled, Freeman exploited the conditions to the full. Immediately he had Hobbs caught, and then bowled Ducat and had Shepherd lbw. He finished with 7 for 43 and took 5 for 112 when Surrey followed on. Even in the return game at The

Oval, Rushby's benefit match, when 1262 runs were scored for the loss of only 27 wickets and five hundreds were hit, Freeman came out with figures of 4 for 117.

It was Gloucestershire and Sussex, however, who felt his venomous spin most acutely. The first game with Gloucestershire was played at Tonbridge in mid-June. Neither side made 140 in an innings, but Kent won by nine wickets. Opening the bowling in the second innings, Freeman took 7 for 35, including six of the first seven. A month later, at Tunbridge Wells, he took 6 for 35 and 6 for 36 to give Kent a nine-wicket victory over Sussex in another low-scoring match. It is interesting to note that Maurice Tate, who bowled four more overs in the match than Freeman, took 8 for 67 and 1 for 19, and Tate was blessed with better support bowling than Freeman.

With two matches of the season remaining, Freeman had taken 165 wickets. The record for a Kent bowler was 185 by Colin Blythe, but records were never foremost in 'Tich' Freeman's mind. He was paid to play cricket, to take wickets. It was on the cricket field that he expressed himself and his method of expression was to toss the ball in the air, now the leg-spinner, now the top-spinner, now the googly, and to lure the batsman to destruction.

The penultimate game of the season was at Cheltenham, the happy hunting ground of Charlie Parker, the slow left-arm bowler whose treatment by England selectors made even their treatment of 'Tich' look good in comparison. Parker took 6 for 82 in this match, but he had to give best to Freeman. The little man's spin was twice too much for Gloucestershire who were beaten by an innings. He had 6 for 18 and 6 for 54. In the second innings he had the assistance of a damp wicket, but his 6 for 18 was taken on a wicket on which Kent later had little difficulty in reaching 248 for 9 declared. So Kent journeyed to Brighton in good heart for the last game of the season.

Sussex had not enjoyed a good season, but few were prepared for what was to happen at Brighton on the last two days of August and the first of September, 1922. After all, the Sussex side did include Tate, the two Gilligans, V. W. C. Jupp, Cox, Bowley and Vine.

What Freeman achieved in this match is of the legend of cricket. With Laker's 19 wickets at Old Trafford, Blythe and Verity taking 17 wickets in a day, and Verity's 10 for 10, his performance at Brighton is to be considered among the very greatest of bowling feats. As *Wisden*, not prone to praise bowlers, expressed it, 'Beyond everything else the bowling of Freeman stood out by itself. In the whole match he took 17 wickets for 67 runs – an astonishing performance, much as rain had affected the pitch. His nine wickets for 11 runs in the first innings was altogether out of the common even among the many feats of bowlers getting rid of nine or ten men in one innings.'

There was only 50 minutes play possible on the Wednesday, but the Sussex first innings was all over after a further 20 minutes on the Thursday. Collins and Woolley opened the bowling, but Collins bowled only one over in which he conceded six runs before giving way to Freeman. Bowley and Vine had started in aggressive vein and 25 were on the board before Vine was taken at slip by Collins off a Freeman leg-break. Immediately Mr R. A. Young, who was the leading Sussex batsman that year, was lured forward and Hubble stumped him. The remaining Sussex batsmen rushed, like lemmings, to destruction. They had been 25 for 0; when Freeman dismissed A. E. R. Gilligan they were 47 for 9. His figures were $10 - 4 - 11 - 9$. With the first ball of his next over Frank Woolley bowled Street, the Sussex no. 10, to rob Freeman of a record which might have stood second only to Verity's at Leeds ten years later. Kent declared at 196 for 9 and Freeman opened the bowling in the second innings, bowling unchanged to take 8 for 56 in 23.5 overs. Bowley and Roberts were the only batsmen to show resistance; they both made 31. Bowley, who had been top scorer in the first innings with 24, was finally bowled by Freeman when he played no shot at a ball pitched just outside off stump – he did not wish to give those vultures at slip another offering. Unfortunately he had mis-read the delivery, a googly, which turned back and bowled him.

In the last week of the season Freeman had taken 29 wickets for 138 runs, a phenomenal performance. No Kent bowler had ever taken more wickets in a season than he had with his 194. Kent were fourth in the County Championship and, in *Wisden 1923*, Alfred Percy Freeman was named one of the Five Cricketers of the Year, an accolade that comes to few cricketers. Yet even the honour bestowed upon him by *Wisden* was tempered with a certain lack of generosity. 'There is no getting away from the fact,' wrote Sydney Pardon, 'that when the chance came to prove himself something more than a county bowler he failed. He was quite harmless against the Australians at Canterbury and had no length against the Gentlemen at The Oval.' This, of course, was a reference to the 1921 season, but it was apparent that an unjustified opinion was being formed that Freeman was ineffective against the best batsmen and, possibly, that he did not have a big-match temperament. The facts did not bear out this judgement.

Against the Australians at Canterbury in 1921 Woolley had been withdrawn from the attack in order to give him a rest and not overbowl him. Freeman had bowled on a perfect wicket against the best batting side in the world who had been intent merely on batting practice. He had taken three wickets for the Players who had won by an innings and had been one of the bowlers responsible for their win against the clock.

In 1922 Freeman was fifth in the first-class averages of regular bowlers and only Charlie Parker took more wickets. At Maidstone he had taken eight wickets in the Yorkshire first innings, during which he passed 100 wickets for the season. His victims had included such as Leyland, Oldroyd, Robinson, Kilner, Holmes and Rhodes. Yorkshire were to become county champions. During the season he had accounted for Hobbs, Russell, Hallows, Makepeace, George Gunn, Quaife, Douglas, Calthorpe, Whysall, Sharp, E. Tyldesley – and yet he did not appear for the Players in any of the three matches against the Gentlemen, nor did he play for the Rest of England against the Champion County, nor was he in the party that was selected to go to South Africa for the Test series under F. T. Mann's leadership.

Once more it was Fender and Stevens who had the leg-spin places, although Stevens was bowling to much less effect at this time. Fender was always a great player. Woolley and Jupp were the other spinners in the party. As it transpired, it was Macaulay and Kennedy who were England's dominant bowlers in the series which saw England win two Tests and South Africa one, with two left drawn. Stevens bowled four overs in the first Test and did not play in the remaining four. Having startled the world with their googly quartet 15 years previously, the South Africans could find no leg-spinner of Test class for this series.

There was a consolation for Freeman. While the MCC were touring South Africa, another MCC side was sent to Australia and New Zealand. The party consisted of 12 amateurs plus Freeman and Harry Tyldesley, who had taken only four wickets in first-class cricket, but was thought to be a leg-break bowler of promise. The captain was A. C. MacLaren, 51 years old and to play his last first-class match on this tour. One selection of great interest was Mr A. P. F. Chapman of Berkshire, 'the hero of the trip,' according to *Wisden*, everyone, both in New Zealand and Australia, being delighted with his brilliant batting and fielding'. The main purpose of the tour was to encourage the rising standard of cricket in New Zealand, and the MCC party included T. C. Lowry of Cambridge University who was later to play for Somerset and to captain New Zealand.

The party first landed in Perth where a two-day game against Western Australia, not then of first-class status, saw Chapman whirl his bat to the entertainment of the crowd and Freeman take 4 for 101. From there the party moved to Adelaide to take on the might of South Australia. The MCC side was not really strong enough to cope with opposition of his nature and was outplayed from start to finish. The state side hit 442 in their first innings, Freeman taking three for 169. The two openers, V. Y. and A. J. Richardson, both to become Test players, hit centuries. MCC were bowled out for 205 and 294, leaving South Australia less than half an hour to get the 58 they needed for victory. Freeman and Tyldesley opened the bowling and with the score at 42 'Tich' sent back A. J. Richardson, V. Y. Richardson and Dolling to record the second hat-trick of his career. His final analysis was quite remarkable: 2 overs, 23 runs, 4 wickets (they were, of course, eight-ball overs). South Australia reached their target for the loss of these four wickets off 33 balls in 21 minutes. Freeman had come out of it well.

He bowled with commendable accuracy in Melbourne, where MCC lost by two wickets to a Victorian side that included Park, Woodfull, Hartkopf, Ellis, Ransford and Grimmett, the first time that the two great leg-spinners were opposed to each other. They each took two wickets in the match, Park and Hartkopf falling to the Englishman. Having met Grimmett for the first time, 'Tich' renewed acquaintance with Mailey in Sydney, where a very strong New South Wales side won by five wickets. Mailey had match figures of 2 for 123; Freeman 2 for 77. He got both openers, Bardsley and Collins, for 6 and 24 respectively. Now for the less rigorous demands of New Zealand.

Freeman did not play in New Zealand until the first of the representative matches which was played in Wellington on 30 December 1922 and 1 and 2 January 1923. At the time it was dignified by the name 'Test match', but that status has not been accorded to the three representative matches since. The game attracted much attention and large crowds in New Zealand, with over 11,000 watching the first two days. MCC won by an innings and 156 runs. The match will be remembered not only for the excitement and interest it stimulated in New Zealand, but also for the fact that in what was to prove his last first-class innings, A. C. MacLaren scored 200 not out, reaching his double century when A. P. Freeman was at the wicket with him. Facing a total of 505 for 8 declared, New Zealand found the bowling of Freeman altogether too good for them. He sent down 72 overs in the match and took 10 for 186 (5 for 114 and 5 for 72). He twice dismissed R. C. Blunt who, ten years later, was to hit a triple century in an inter-provincial match.

In the second 'Test' the England bowling was mastered by the New Zealanders for the only time on the tour. Freeman himself bowled economically and took four wickets in the drawn game in which honours went to the home side. Freeman's 14 runs at no.

11 gave MCC a surprise first-innings lead of nine runs. He was in good form against Otago and Minor Associations and in the third of the representative games he played a big part in MCC's victory. Gibson and Calthorpe did the bowling in the first innings and then Lowry hit a hundred against his own countrymen to put MCC well on top. In the second New Zealand innings Freeman tore the heart out of the batting when, coming into the attack after Collins and Blunt had made a fine opening stand, he caught Blunt and then took four wickets for 95 in a spell of 40 overs. One of those to fall to him was Dacre, later to join Gloucestershire. 'Tich's' farewell to New Zealand was 12 wickets against Auckland.

On the return through Australia he had splendid matches against New South Wales and South Australia, and 0 for 121 against Victoria when Victoria made 617 for 6 after bowling out MCC for 71 and then were denied victory when Hill-Wood and Maclean scored centuries and batted out the last day. In all matches in Australia and New Zealand he had taken 82 wickets, and in first-class matches 69 wickets at 24 runs each. He was by far the most telling wicket-taker in the side. In Australia, on the finest of wickets, he had puzzled and dismissed some of the greatest batsmen in the world; Pellew, Vic Richardson, Collins, Bardsley, Andrews, Macartney had all succumbed to him. *Wisden* agreed he was the mainstay of the side but felt that he had not proved half as destructive on New Zealand wickets as had been expected. In many ways they were underestimating both the opposition and the wickets.

The Kent googly bowler could be well pleased with his first tour and must have felt that he was on the threshold of a Test career. There were to be no Test matches in 1923, since the West Indies were touring and they had not attained Test status, but there were to be six matches of a Test trial nature. 'Tich' Freeman did not play in one of them.

5
Out in the Cold,
1923–24

The season 1923 was a difficult one for Kent for although they dropped only one place in the County Championship, finishing fifth, there was a growing realisation that all the bowling was coming increasingly to rest on the shoulders of 'Tich' Freeman. The decline in Frank Woolley's potency as a spinner became very obvious; as he still took just over 100 wickets in all matches, this seems a harsh judgement by today's standards, but in county games his capacity for taking wickets dropped dramatically. He took 89 wickets for Kent and his ability to turn the ball faded fast during the season. Ashdown, Wright and, in particular, Collins gave able support, but in match after match Freeman was having to be used as the one bowler likely to get the other side out. It was not something that bothered him, for his sole happiness was in the art of bowling.

He took fewer wickets than he had done the previous year, finishing with 157, but only Rhodes, Kilner, Macaulay, Tate, Matthews, J. C. White and R. Tyldesley of those bowlers who reached 100 wickets got them at a cheaper cost. He bowled in 24 innings before he failed to take a wicket, against Warwickshire at Edgbaston at the beginning of July. A fortnight later he failed to take a wicket in the first innings against Essex when he bowled only seven overs, but in the remaining 25 innings of the season in which he bowled, at least one batsman fell to him each time. Surprisingly, he frequently came much later into the attack than he had done in previous seasons, Collins, Captain Cornwallis, Wright, Woolley, Hardinge or Ashdown often preceding him. Yet still he monopolised the wicket-taking, and Hobbs, Holmes, Makepeace, Mead, Stevens, Whysall, Harry Altham and the young Wally Hammond were among those who fell to him cheaply. R. E. S. Wyatt was dismissed for 1 and 2 at Dover, both times by Freeman who had 14 for 161 in the match and yet saw his side beaten.

Kent beat the touring West Indies with ease at Canterbury, 'Tich' bowling only 10.1 overs in the match but taking three wickets. With no Test matches to be played against the West Indies it was decided to hold Test trials. The three Gentlemen v. Players matches and the Champion County v. the Rest of England were always in the nature of important representative matches, both honouring and testing. To them were added two official Test trials, North v. South and England v. The Rest.

A special sub-committee was set up to pick the sides for these two trials for which professionals were to be paid £16 if selected, a good sum by the financial standards of cricketers in those days. The committee was chaired by H. D. G. Leveson-Gower and the other two members were the Somerset captain, John Daniell, and Lionel Troughton. The latter had first played for Kent in 1907 and handed over the captaincy of Kent to Captain (later Lord) Cornwallis in 1923. Troughton himself took over the post of business manager of Kent that year when the beloved and devoted Tom Pawley died at Canterbury at the beginning of August. Lionel Troughton was a big influence on 'Tich' in his early days in the Kent side. It was Troughton who set Freeman's field for him, discussing and explaining what he was doing. He handled the leg-spinner with tact and firmness and he taught him much. Above all he told him much about the weaknesses of opposing batsmen and how to discover those weaknesses for himself. There were those who believed that Freeman missed this positive direction when playing under a captain from another county.

Lieutenant-Colonel Troughton may have captained 'Tich' in palmy days, but evidently his influence went for little because the Kent googly bowler played in none of the representative matches that year. Troughton himself may have believed that Freeman was not yet ready without his guidance, and this belief would have been founded on concern for the man, not from any arrogance of Troughton's.

As it was, Fender played in the representative matches, of course, as did J. W. Hearne, Stevens and now Richard Tyldesley; even Richmond, still able to impart considerable spin but nearing Falstaffian proportions, was recalled. It was all very strange, but then so was much concerning the non-selection of Alfred Percy Freeman.

1923 was, in fact, a somewhat bizarre year for him. The game with Lancashire at Gravesend on the last days of May and the first of June was marked by Parkin bowling his off-spin to a leg trap of four men. It was memorable, too, for the fact that in Kent's second innings Freeman hit a ball from Richard Tyldesley over the pavilion, so revenging what had been done to him the previous season and at the same time putting one of his rivals firmly in his place. He scored 2? that day. At Leicester, in another game that Kent lost, he was facing George Geary in the second innings when he played and missed and the ball hit the off-stump, going on to the boundary for four byes. The off bail had been removed from the groove but did not fall. On this occasion the batsman did not last very much longer.

It was in the final game of the season, at Lord's, however, that the most singular incident befell him. There had been no play on the first day of the match due to rain, but when Kent batted the wicket did not prove as treacherous as many had feared. The middle order, nevertheless, surrendered lamely to Lee and Allen, but the Kent tail wagged viciously and 'Tich' was enjoying himself in a stand with Captain Cornwallis. The first ball of an over from Stevens had been played to the leg boundary where it was fielded by Dales. As the batsmen went through for a run Dales threw to the wicket and the ball, bouncing once, hit Freeman on the head. He was knocked unconscious and big Jack Durston carried the little man from the field in his arms, a sight to rival Lear's entrance with Cordelia. He quickly recovered, but the doctor who examined him ordered that he should take no more part in the match. It was, perhaps, a fitting end to 1923.

In fact it was not quite the end. Kent made a short tour of Scotland in September and, not unexpectedly, the opposition found A. P. Freeman a little too much for them. At Mannofield he was opposed to the great Albert Vogler, one of the South African googly masters, who took 14 Kent wickets in the match in which Aberdeenshire gained an honourable draw. At Inverness the North of Scotland's opening bat hit Freeman out of the ground, then was bowled next ball. He had scored seven. Hell hath no fury like a spinner scorn'd.

The following season, 1924, began with the now customary personal triumphs, but personalities and incidents outside Freeman himself were to have some bearing on his future. Percy Chapman and 'Father' Marriott made their first appearances for Kent in 1924. Chapman was to become Freeman's skipper and C. S. Marriott was to link with him in the deadliest leg-break combination that English county cricket was ever to know. The other personality played for Lancashire. His name was Cecil Parkin and 1924 saw the end of his Test career.

The South Africans were touring this summer and Parkin and Richard Tyldesley had routed them in the game with Lancashire at Old Trafford. Parkin was in wonderful form and took 200 wickets at under 14 runs each during the season. The first Test was played at Birmingham and the spin was in the hands of Parkin, Woolley, Kilner and Fender. Taylor of South Africa won the toss and asked England to bat on what was believed to be a rain-affected wicket. England scored 438 and when South Africa batted Gilligan and Tate disposed of them in 12.3 overs for 30. In the follow-on South Africa scored 390; Tate bowled 54.4 overs, Gilligan 28 and Parkin 16.

At this time an article used to appear regularly under Parkin's name in a Sunday newspaper. On the Sunday following the Test it was published with a banner headline, 'Cecil Parkin Refuses to Play for England Again'. It contained statements to the effect that while Gilligan had been ringing the changes in the second innings in an effort to get rid of Catterall, who scored a hundred, Parkin had been overlooked. Parkin, it was said, had never felt so humiliated in the whole course of his cricket career and, he emphasised, 'I am not going to stand being treated as I was on Tuesday'. Parkin later asserted that the article had been 'ghosted' for him and that, as he had been rushing from Gloucester to Ashby-de-la Zouch after a county game, he had had no previous knowledge of what was to appear. His protestations were in vain. Overnight the most popular of cricketers, renowned for his comic antics in flicking the ball from foot to hand and hiding it in his pocket, had become the most unpopular. His representative career was over and two years later he left county cricket.

In passing, it is worth noting that Parkin had the very highest regard for Freeman. He considered that there were only two great googly bowlers in the world, Mailey, whom he ranked first, and Freeman. This was his assessment in 1936 when, looking back on that golden age which is always just out of sight, he contended that the greatest of English bowlers had been Barnes, Hirst, Rhodes, Walter Brearley, Frank Foster and 'Tich' Freeman. Larwood, he thought, was 'a five-over bowler'. What Parkin looked for in a bowler was individuality and he saw that in Freeman as he saw it in Barnes and the rest. He was vehement in refuting the opinion that Freeman was ineffective against the best batsmen: ' . . . some folk are grudging in their praise of his work. They say, ''Freeman's victims are mostly 'rabbits'.'' Stuff and nonsense. ''Tich'' is a wonderful chap. There may be a lot of ''rabbits'' among the batsmen in first-class cricket, but there are not nearly so many as that statement suggests, neither do they always fall to the same bowler year after year.'

Freeman did not play in the Test trial in May 1924, nor did he appear in any of the Test matches. There were two other leg-break bowlers, J. W. Hearne and Richard Tyldesley, who came in for

Parkin and Kilner. A week after the third Test, however, was the Gentlemen v. Players match at Lord's. For this game, 'The MCC Committee were able to select for each side exactly the men they wanted, and only in one or two particulars were the teams open to criticism.' As *Wisden* went on to point out, 'On his form Parkin was clearly entitled to be picked for the Players, but by reason of his having rushed into print with his grievances after the Test match at Birmingham he had put himself out of court.' Freeman did play, and so once more the way was open for him to prove himself at the top level.

The Players won the toss and with Hobbs and Kilner hitting hundreds and Hearne and Tate reaching fifty, they totalled 514. Freeman batted no. 9 and scored 19. It should be remembered that the Gentlemen's attack was a formidable one – Douglas, Robertson-Glasgow, Gilligan, Fender, J. C. White and Stevens, though Fender retired from the attack with a strained back muscle. On a perfect batting wicket the Gentlemen were expected to accomplish a draw with ease, a win in face of the record total being out of the question. Howell, the Warwickshire bowler who had been badly let down by his fielders when he toured Australia in 1920–21, bowled very quickly and dismissed the openers, MacBryan and J. L. Bryan. Freeman was brought on to replace Tate and immediately pitched on a length and spun the ball to such effect that in no time the Gentlemen were in disarray at 66 for 6. Gilligan hit 33 out of 36 in 20 minutes, but this was only a temporary setback to the Players. The Gentlemen were out for 130 and Freeman had taken the wickets of Stevens, Carr, M. K. Foster, M. D. Lyon, Gilligan and J. C. White, nos. 3 to 8 in the batting order, at a cost of 52 runs on a perfect pitch. Rain fell to make the wicket a difficult one when the Gentlemen followed on. Freeman dismissed both openers and then Kilner exploited the drying pitch to give the Players an overwhelming victory

Kilner had obviously had a splendid match, but Freeman's wickets had come against the best of amateur batting on a wicket which gave the bowler no assistance. In his history of the Gentlemen v. Players matches, written a quarter of a century after this match, Sir Pelham Warner praises the bowling of Kilner, Douglas and Robertson-Glasgow and the batting of Hobbs, Kilner and Stevens; Freeman is not mentioned. Sir Pelham Warner was a very powerful figure in cricket in the second quarter of this century – is there here some clue to why Freeman was so often passed over for representative honours?

The performance of the Kent leg-break and googly bowler could not be ignored, however. His county finished fifth in the Championship and his contribution received fulsome praise from Lord Harris in the annual report to members: 'On Freeman the Eleven largely depended for successful attack in bowling. He kept a most accurate length, displayed great judgment, and has a fine record for the Season.' But the most salient comment was to be found in *Wisden*: 'Freeman was the mainstay of the Kent bowling, taking 146 wickets in county matches for less than fifteen and a half runs each, and putting everyone else in the shade. He retained all his spin and could still vary his leg-breaks now and then with a genuine googly. Over and above what he did in county cricket, he had a startling success in the Gentlemen and Players' match at Lord's, this probably turning the scale in his favour when the time came for the MCC to choose their team for Australia. He was one of the most consistent of slow bowlers last summer, coming off in match after match.'

So 'Tich' stood within a pace of becoming a Test player as he departed for Australia with the MCC side at the end of 1924, and yet his selection had not been greeted with universal approval. There was no Macaulay, no Parkin (inevitably), and no White. Freeman was not an extrovert character who won the approval of pressmen and spectators with the instant histrionics of a Parkin or, latterly, a Greig or a Randall. He was a quiet man whose character was in his bowling. His response to a bad decision or a streaky four was a hitch of the trousers with the forearms in a manner that was to become entirely his own and a shrug which meant 'watch out next ball'. He lived for bowling and the impostors of triumph and disaster were treated with equal disdain. He was in many respects a paradox: the records that he accumulated were accepted with the

indifference of one who believed that they were an inevitable part
of the job he was paid to do, and yet there was a diffidence as if he
could not understand, in his humility, how he was vying with
these great men.

6

Australia Again, 1924–25

The 1924–25 series in Australia saw Hobbs and Sutcliffe batting together in a Test match against Australia for the first time. In his first Test series Sutcliffe scored 734 runs and became the first man to score four centuries in a Test rubber. Ponsford, A. J. and V. Y. Richardson, Hartkopf, Whysall, Kippax and, sensationally in the last match, Grimmett all made their debuts in Test cricket. For the first time eight-ball overs were bowled in Test cricket and for the first time a Test match lasted seven days; each of the first three Tests, in fact, ended on the seventh day. In a series in which batsmen dominated on hard, true wickets – there were no less than 14 centuries scored during the series and Ryder's 201 stood as an Australian record against England in Australia until Bradman broke it over 12 years later – Maurice Tate set an English record with 38 wickets. Nevertheless, for the third series in succession England were overwhelmed, losing by four Tests to one. Whoever won the toss won the match.

The *Sydney Sunday News* estimated that England dropped 21 catches in the series (they thought that Australia dropped three more than England) and that the dropped catches cost England 576 runs. Such a reckoning is, of course, pure conjecture, but more than any other factor, dropped catches had also contributed to England's downfall on the previous tour. This weakness in catching is something of a surprise, for the MCC team was under the leadership of Arthur Edward Robert Gilligan, a likeable and enthusiastic man who placed much importance on ability in the field. Gilligan had had considerable success as England's leader against South Africa, taking 6 for 7 in that Test which was to be Parkin's last. A few weeks later he was struck over the heart while batting, ordered to rest and was never the same bowler again; the series in which he led England in Australia was to mark the end of his Test career.

The series, too, was to see the end of J. W. H. T. Douglas as a Test player. He had captained England in the first seven Test matches after the war, all of which they had lost, but he was a man of tenacity and courage whom history has treated badly. The two other amateurs in the party were Percy Chapman, soon to become the hero of English cricket, and another Kent left-hander, J. L. Bryan, an exciting batsman destined never to play Test cricket and to be lost to business.

Douglas was the only one of the four amateurs to have toured Australia before. Hobbs, Strudwick, Hendren, Howell, Woolley and Hearne had made previous visits, but Andy Sandham, Dick Tyldesley, Tate, Sutcliffe, Kilner, 'Dodger' Whysall (a surprise choice as deputy wicket-keeper, Duckworth or M. D. Lyon having been expected to make the trip), and Freeman were touring Australia with a full England side for the first time.

Of the 17 players in the party, three were leg-break and googly bowlers.

On any Test tour a cricketer is confronted with the problem of establishing himself in the side before the first Test, for success after that time may have come too late. If a side wins the first Test on tour, those in the side have achieved a certain amount of immunity from replacement for the rest of the series. Today we are used to the problem of an unleavened diet of Test cricket, but the 1924–25 tour presented a comparable lack of variety at times. The first and second Tests followed one upon the other, and the second Test was separated from the third only by a game against a Ballarat XV.

'Tich' did not play in the opening match against Western Australia and met with moderate success in a two-day game against Western Australian Colts, a side which included Mervyn Inverarity, father of John who was destined to lead the state to greatness. The return game with Western Australia, a four-day match, was treated more seriously. Gilligan hit a century and MCC reached 397. There was a little overnight rain but Western Australia, not then a strong side, batted on a good wicket. They made a fair start against Tate, Gilligan, Howell and Douglas, but the introduction of Freeman into the attack changed the complexion of the innings. Monty Noble wrote later: 'Freeman bowled splendidly. His length was always good and he turned the ball considerably, an occasional ''wrong'un'' mystifying the batsmen.' At one time he had 4 for 11 and he finished with 6 for 47, the six victims being from the first eight in the order. When the home state followed on he took 3 for 23 and MCC won by an innings. The Australians must have been in a hurry to get home as three of them were run out in an innings which totalled only 69. Freeman had grabbed his first chance, and he enjoyed himself again in the match at Kalgoorlie against the Goldfields Association, a minor match in which, once more, he 'mystified' the opposition. Despite this, he missed selection for the first important match of the tour, with South Australia at Adelaide Oval. MCC won this game by nine wickets, although they were helped by a first-innings declaration when South Australia seemed on their way to amassing a huge score. Tyldesley failed to take a wicket in this match, but Jack Hearne, who had not shown his best form in the earlier matches, took advantage of slight help from the pitch in the second innings to take 5 for 17. Clarrie Grimmett bowled most impressively for South Australia.

There followed defeat at the hands of Victoria. This was a disappointment to a side which had shown such encouraging form at the start of the tour. An injured knee put Hearne out of the match after the first innings and this was a great handicap, but generally the batting failed to produce the necessary sparkle. 'Tich' bowled well, taking the wickets of Hendry, Ponsford and Hartkopf, all of

55

whom were to represent Australia during the Test series, for 37 runs.

It is worth, perhaps, quoting one incident from the match. In his book, *Gilligan's Men*, Monty Noble recalls: 'I noticed a delightful little incident that filled me with pride for the triumph of the sporting instinct. Freeman received a severe blow on the leg in stopping a hard return from Mayne. It was evidently very painful and he might easily have wasted time over it – very valuable time then – but, instead, he limped along and sent down a rather easy one to Woodfull. The latter could well have punished it, but, instead, he played it to the off for the value of about a single and refused to run. Many of the spectators missed the point and wondered why a few hearty cheers went up. That was cricket!'

Noble's point is, of course, concerned with Woodfull's sportsmanship which he compares with a similar action of Hobbs in the third Test of 1909, but the incident reveals something about Freeman, too. In all his cricket career he accepted pain as he accepted disappointment – unquestioningly and uncomplainingly. He just got on with the job. The knock affected him, but before it, Noble says, he 'troubled all the batsmen with his slows. He turned from the leg, bowled his over-spin with great accuracy, and was always difficult.'

'Tich' did not play in the triumph over New South Wales in which Tyldesley bowled well, but returned for the match in Brisbane. MCC held the upper hand in this game which was not considered as being of the greatest importance for, at that time, Queensland had not attained Sheffield Shield status. It turned out to be a good game for Freeman, however, and in retrospect an important one. He and Dick Tyldesley added 54 for the last wicket and when Queensland batted on a perfect pitch, 'Tyldesley and Freeman had to be called in to apply the brake'. When the home side batted again, to quote Noble again, 'Freeman again puzzled the batsmen, but Tyldesley was much less effective'. The important factor was his effectiveness on an excellent wicket – he took 5 for 128 in the match – when only Tate of the other bowlers seemed to have the same ability. Percy Hornibrook, who was on the verge of the Australian side and was later to play six times for his country, took 5 for 210 in the 34 overs he bowled in the England innings.

The MCC stayed in Brisbane for the game against an Australian XI, a flexing of muscles before the real contest began. Again the wicket was perfect and runs came at an inflationary rate. 'Tich' bowled quite splendidly in an innings that lasted nine hours. He sent down 35 overs and took 6 for 160. He always looked dangerous and troubled the batsman with both the top-spinner and the googly. Tyldesley also bowled well, but according to Noble, 'none of the others looked like getting wickets'. It is worth comparing Freeman's figures with Grimmett's in the same match: in the MCC innings the Australian bowled one more over than 'Tich' had done in the Australian first innings and took the wickets of Douglas, Bryan, Chapman (stumped for 92) and Tyldesley for 176 runs.

The second innings of the Australian XI dissolved in farce as Douglas, who was captaining the MCC side, gave every member of his team a turn with the ball. When Herbert Strudwick came on to bowl 'Tich' went behind the stumps. Ron Oxenham jumped out at Strudwick and missed. 'Tich' whipped off the bails and recorded the only stumping of his first-class career. In the first innings Oxenham had been deceived by a Freeman googly and stumped and so, possibly uniquely in first-class cricket, we have the record:

(1st inns) R. K. Oxenham st Strudwick, b Freeman 54
(2nd inns) R. K. Oxenham st Freeman, b Strudwick 0

Under more conventional circumstances, 'Tich' was always a good fielder. He was an alert and safe cover and, on occasions, a reliable slip.

There remained only two minor matches before the first Test. When one looks at the composition of the sides for these two matches one realises that the only doubt in the minds of the selectors must have been whether or not Woolley would be fit to replace Kilner. At Toowoomba and against Australian Juniors at

Sydney 'Tich' again bamboozled the opposition. The Juniors were led by the veteran Monty Noble, but none of them ever appears to have graduated into becoming a senior.

So Alfred Percy Freeman took the field as an England player for the first time. He was 36 years old. Most people agreed with the selection of the England side although there was a feeling that a place should have been found for Kilner, a valuable late-order left-hander, possibly at the expense of Sandham, an opener who found himself at no. 6.

Collins won the toss and he and Bardsley faced the bowling of Gilligan and Tate on a splendid wicket. There was a crowd of 47,000 at Sydney for the first day of this game and Australia proceeded at an easy pace against the opening bowling. The first change in the attack was made when Gilligan replaced himself by Freeman. Bardsley had made 21 out of 46 when he tried to drive Freeman through the covers. The ball was pitched well up outside the off stump and was, in all probability, the googly which to the left-hander became the leg-break. It took the outside edge and Woolley held a comfortable catch at slip. It was a long time before England had another success. The Australian innings lasted for 8½ hours and totalled 450. Freeman dismissed Vic Richardson for 42 and bowled 49 overs, 11 of which were maidens, to take 2 for 124.

England reached 298, but only four of their batsmen reached double figures: Hobbs 115, Hendren 74 not out, Sutcliffe 59 and Chapman 13. Freeman was bowled by Gregory for 0. It is interesting to record that Arthur Mailey took four wickets but, in bowling 18 overs fewer than Freeman, he conceded five runs more.

Freeman and Tate had carried the England bowling on their shoulders and did so again in the second innings although this time with a little more support. Arthur Richardson opened the second innings with Bardsley, Collins being compelled to miss part of the match through a family bereavement, and played an aggressive innings. He reached 98 before he failed to reach the pitch of a ball from Freeman and gave the little man a return catch, his first in Test cricket.

Ponsford was looking as if he would make a big score when one of 'Tich's' leg-breaks turned enough to take the outside edge for Frank Woolley to hold a fine catch low down to his right at slip. The Kent combination also accounted for Gregory. A last-wicket stand of 127 between Mailey and Taylor, a record against England which still stands, frustrated the tourists and threw some doubts on Gilligan's tactics in the use of his bowlers.

Freeman had sent down 37 overs and his three wickets had cost 134 runs. It was a most creditable performance. Hearne had retired from the attack with a damaged hand in the first innings and was obviously below his best in the second innings. Woolley was not used at all in the second innings when Australia made 452 and the responsibility placed on Freeman meant that on a perfect wicket he was both the only attacking spinner and the only stock bowler. As Noble commented, 'Freeman, as in the first innings, was a very useful foil between Gilligan and Tate. He had to do a lot of hard work, and kept a wonderful length for a slow bowler.'

In view of this comment and his assessment of Freeman at other times during the tour, Noble's diary note at the end of the Test that 'Freeman is not a leg-break bowler, but bowls what is called a "straight break" with over spin, and sometimes bowls a ball with the suspicion of a wrong 'un. He keeps a good length, has great staying power, fields well, and is a better bat than most people imagine' is a little puzzling, but it would appear to suggest that 'Tich' had been forced into the position of relying mainly on the top-spinner, partly because of the placidity of the wicket, but mainly because of the role he was asked to adopt.

None who played against him would ever agree with Noble's statement that 'Tich' was not a leg-break bowler, but it is certainly true that his success in county cricket was due to the fact that he turned the ball just enough on the average county pitch. There were other leg-spinners who turned the ball more, but with much less success, beating the bat and the wicket; 'Tich' nearly always hit the wicket or the edge of the bat if the batsman did not hit him. But because he did not turn the ball as much as other leg-spinners, the Australians, in Australia, decided to play him as a 'straight' bowler. They were not afraid to use their feet to him. He responded by pushing the ball through more quickly and lost some of his flight in consequence. The 'bush telegraph' of first-class cricket suggested that this would be the case in England. His achievement does not support that view, but it is hard to change opinions once they have taken root.

In addition Jack Bryan, who was a member of the England party on this tour, confirms how much Freeman owed to Lionel Troughton who, as we have seen, set his field for him and taught him a great deal about the opposing batsmen and how to bowl to them. Gilligan was a sympathetic and intelligent leader, but he was never in a position to give 'Tich' the same degree of attention, and it is certain that Freeman missed this direction.

England began their second innings needing 605 to win and Hobbs and Sutcliffe joined together in the first of their century opening partnerships in a Test match against Australia; they had shared in big stands against South Africa a few months previously. Once more, however, the England batting was dreadfully inconsistent, and Hearne, Hendren, Sandham, Tate and Gilligan scored only 12 between them.

When Freeman joined Frank Woolley England were 276 for 8 and the match was as good as over, but when stumps were drawn at the end of that sixth day both batsmen were still there and the score was 362. There was an unusual incident when, after the umpires had pulled up the stumps at six o'clock, Collins and Gilligan held a conference on the field, stopping the players on their way back to the pavilion, and play was resumed for another quarter of an hour, presumably in an attempt to finish the match that night. The Kent men did not co-operate in achieving that object.

The next morning Frank Woolley, who was still troubled by his injured knee, reached a magnificent hundred. He had scored 123 when he failed to get far enough across to a ball from Gregory that moved away a little and he edged to Mailey in the slips. The Kent pair had added 128 for the ninth wicket, which remains the second highest for this England wicket against Australia, bettered only by the 151 of Walter Read and William Scotton at The Oval in 1884.

Strudwick stayed just long enough for 'Tich' to reach his maiden fifty in first-class cricket in his first Test match. It was a courageous innings – it was the man. He played some cover drives that brother Jack would have envied, and his application put some of the specialist batsmen in the side to shame.

Freeman could feel well pleased with his debut. Apart from his batting he had sent down 688 balls and dismissed five of the leading Australian batsmen for 258 runs in a match in which six centuries had been scored and in which batsmen, on a beautiful wicket, had no worries about time. The Australian record-holder, Arthur Mailey, had sent down 504 balls and conceded 308 runs for his seven wickets.

The Australians brought in Hartkopf, another leg-break bowler, for the second Test and left out the medium-pace Hendry. England dropped Freeman. As *Wisden* put it, 'Douglas and Richard Tyldesley were included in the England side instead of Sandham and Freeman, but again Kilner was left out. The changes did not strengthen the side, Douglas taking but one wicket and Tyldesley proving quite ineffective.' In comparing the respective Test records of Freeman and Tyldesley it is beyond comprehension how the Lancastrian was ever preferred, yet he was, even six years later when 'Tich' was at the peak of his achievement as a record wicket-taker in county cricket. Certainly Richard Tyldesley was a good bowler who spun the ball more than 'Tich', but rarely to such effect.

Australia won the second Test with ease. They scored 600 in the first innings after being 47 for 3. Hobbs and Sutcliffe put on 283 for the first wicket, both scoring centuries, and Sutcliffe scored a second hundred in the next innings, but apart from fifty from Woolley there were no other significant contributions and England lost by 81 runs. Jack Hearne had 4 for 84 in the second Australian innings. Mailey had match figures of 7 for 233.

'Tich' did nothing against the XV of Ballarat whereas Richard Tyldesley took six wickets, but this could hardly be considered as adequate preparation for a Test match and there were three changes in the side for the match at Adelaide: Freeman, Whysall and Kilner came in for Tyldesley, Hearne and Douglas.

Once more Collins won the toss, but Australia faltered at the start. Collins and Arthur Richardson opened and Collins quickly fell to Tate. Gregory came in at no. 3 to provide the left-hand contrast, but Freeman's googly accounted for him with the score at 19 and when Taylor went to Tate Australia were 22 for 3. What followed, however, was most unhappy for England. The records state that Australia made 489 and that Ryder scored 201 not out, going in at no. 7. What the scorecard does not reveal is the chapter of accidents that befell the tourists.

Having taken 2 for 12, Tate was seen limping, apparently in great pain from an injured toe, an old wound. He was later forced to leave the field. Gilligan broke down after the seventh ball of his eighth over. He strained a groin muscle and left the field, Chapman taking over the captaincy. He did not bowl again in the match. Freeman damaged his wrist so badly that he, too, was forced to leave the field for a time, so leaving England without their three front-line bowlers. 'Tich's' final figures in this innings of 1 for 107 in 18 overs can indicate only that after initial success he proved expensive. What they cannot indicate is the handicap under which he bowled, yet these are the figures that condemn him as a Test bowler against Australia. Of such gossamer are legends made.

After a somewhat bizarre rearrangement of the batting order England made 365. At the end of the fourth day Australia were 211 for 3 in their second innings, Freeman having bowled both Collins and Taylor to claim two of the three wickets. Once more the pitch was in perfect condition and to beat and bowl two of the world's leading batsmen was a splendid achievement.

Early on the fifth morning it rained and the start of play was delayed by over three-quarters of an hour before Australia continued their innings on a drying wicket. These must have been the conditions for which 'Tich' had prayed, for he had exploited them to the full so consistently in England over the past five years. Yet, cruelly and unbelievably, he was not asked to bowl. Instead the left-armers, Kilner and Woolley, whose decline as a bowler has already been noted, were given the ball. The last seven Australian wickets fell for an additional 39 runs, and Alfred Percy Freeman's greatest chance had been denied him. There was to be a similar episode four years later.

It is strange how the gods of cricket have their sport with some and not with others. Frank Tyson's first Test match against Australia in 1954–55 gave him figures of 1 for 160 in 29 overs but he was retained to become the scourge of Australia. 'Tich' Freeman was never accorded such sympathy and yet in his context he deserved it more.

England needed 375 to win and Hobbs and Sutcliffe gave them a useful start. Although Chapman and Whysall played good knocks, the wickets fell slowly but surely. It was 312 for 8 when Freeman joined his captain, Gilligan, and with the wicket wearing, an Australian victory by the end of the sixth day seemed certain. Excitement began to mount, however, as Freeman, after a hesitant start, played with authority and determination. At 348 for 8 both batsmen were well set, England were in command and defeat looked out of the question, but rain ended play for the day and tomorrow is rarely the same as today. Gilligan and Freeman had to start all over again against bowlers who were refreshed and a field who sensed that a reprieve had been granted.

Gregory bowled the first over of the seventh morning to Freeman. The first ball went wide of the wicket for four byes. Of the next four balls three were yorkers; two were dealt with comfortably, one gave more trouble as Freeman played and missed. The sixth ball of the over was wide of the off stump and moving across, 'Tich' square-cut it for two. The last two balls were left alone and after the first over of the day England were only 20 behind.

Mailey bowled the second over of the day after much consultation and rearrangement of the field. Gilligan restrained his naturally aggressive instincts and on-drove the fourth ball for single. From the next ball 'Tich' played probably the worst shot of his innings as he looped the ball over Kelleway's head at silly mid-on, but it brought a run and there was another off the seventh ball when Gilligan drove into the covers.

Gregory now began his second over of the morning. Gilligan hit the second ball firmly to mid-off, and the third. He was beaten by the fourth and some superb fielding saved a run off the fifth. The next ball looked the same and once more Gilligan went for the cover drive, but Gregory had held it back a little and the ball lofted to Vic Richardson at mid-off. He jumped in the air, evidently anticipating the ball would be high, but he dropped his hands and held the ball safely.

The ninth wicket had added 45 and Gilligan had batted for 1¾ hours for his 31. It had been a most valiant innings. If only he could have stayed for another ten minutes!

Strudwick survived the rest of the over with two rather fortuitous edges and then it was Mailey to Freeman. The Kent man played with confidence and was cruelly unlucky when a scorching straight drive hit the stumps at the other end and a certain two became nothing. There was no-one on the field who could have stopped Freeman's shot to the seventh ball of the over: Mailey pitched outside off stump and Freeman cracked it through the covers for four.

Strudwick allowed the majority of Gregory's deliveries to pass through to the wicket-keeper, but he pulled the seventh for two. Now England were only eleven behind.

Mailey to Freeman. No stroke. The second ball is just outside off stump. 'Tich' moves across to cut. There is a snick. Oldfield roars as Mailey leaps in the air. Australia have retained the Ashes.

The Australian crowd – a large crowd despite the prospect of very little play – chaired Mailey from the ground; Freeman's wicket had given him 3 for 126. The little man from Kent slumped dejectedly in the dressing room. He never showed emotion, but he was close to tears that day. Had he known that he would never play against Australia again, he might well have wept openly.

Hearne took Freeman's place for the fourth Test, which England won when they won the toss for the only time in the series. Tate and Kilner were the bowling heroes.

In a run-sodden match with New South Wales only Freeman

and Kilner came out with any respectability as bowlers, but Sandham for Chapman was the only change for the last Test. England were totally destroyed by a leg-break bowler who was making his debut in Test cricket, Clarrie Grimmett. He took 11 for 82 in the match, Hearne had 2 for 117, and it is interesting to conjecture what 'Tich' might have done in the conditions.

In his *Cricket Between Two Wars* Sir Pelham Warner wrote, as part of a brief resumé of Freeman's career, 'He was not a success in Australia in the only two Test matches in which he played. I have heard, however, that fortune did not smile on him on those occasions, and that he was a great googly bowler cannot be questioned. Australian pitches are very trying to bowlers of his type. The great South Africans, Vogler, Schwarz and Faulkner, discovered this to their cost, and even Grimmett and Mailey were far more effective here than in their own country.'

That fortune did not smile we have seen, but when we consider the final achievement, was it so disastrous? In four Test innings he had taken eight wickets, all leading batsmen. Woolley had bowled in twice as many innings and captured the same number of wickets, four of those coming on the rain-affected pitch at Adelaide when 'Tich' had been denied a chance to bowl. Gilligan had bowled in nine innings and taken two more wickets than Freeman. The Kent man's eight wickets had cost him 57.37 runs each, which is the figure at which people point the finger of accusation and nod knowingly, but Gilligan's ten wickets had cost him 51.90 each, Hearne's 11 had cost him 49 apiece and Woolley's had been bought for 46.87 each.

The leading wicket-takers on the Australian side were Gregory and Mailey whose averages were 37.09 and 41.62 respectively, and they were the key bowlers in a side which won the series most convincingly, four matches to one. Hartkopf, in what was to be his only Test match, took 1 for 134. He also hit 80, but such was the strength of the Australian batting that he was not needed again.

In all first-class matches on the tour Freeman took 40 wickets at 30.12; Mailey, the pride of Australia, averaged 30.45 and Gregory 34.30 that season. Kilner also took 40 wickets, but he sent down 35 overs more than 'Tich'. Only Tate's splendid 77 wickets stood above these two.

At least 'Tich' had the consolation of finishing third in the Test match batting averages behind Sutcliffe and Hobbs.

Over the next few years Alfred Percy Freeman was to take wickets in first-class cricket at a rate which had never been achieved before and almost certainly will never be achieved again, yet he was never asked to play against Australia again. His failing had been that in two Test matches against one of the strongest batting sides that cricket has ever known he took eight wickets for 459 runs. Four years previously an Australian fast bowler, 'Ted' McDonald, had made his Test debut and in three Tests against a side that had been completely outplayed and badly mauled he took 6 for 392. A few months later McDonald was in England destroying all that was put in his path. Freeman was never accorded such an opportunity. To many, over 50 years ago, this seemed as incomprehensible as it does to us today.

Alfred Percy Freeman – an early picture.

2. The Kent County XI, 1925.
Back row: Wright, Hardinge, Woolley
Middle row: A. P. Day, Captain Cornwallis, S. E. Day, Hubble
Front row: Ashdown, Seymour, Freeman, Collins

3 & 4. Two views of the 'whip' in delivery. Above: v. Surrey at Blackheath, 1932. Below: 14 years later, at the age of 58, for Old England against Surrey at The Oval. Jack Hobbs is umpire and Errol Holmes at mid-on. The batsman is Eric Bedser.

5. Stumped Ames, bowled Freeman was one of the most common of scorebook entries. Here A. C. Rhodes is given the benefit of the doubt, only to be caught Hardinge, bowled Freeman a few balls later.

6. Canterbury in the 1930s.

7. The left arm is thrown high, the batsman is perfectly sighted: Freeman in action against Yorkshire at Tonbridge. Barber is the batsman.

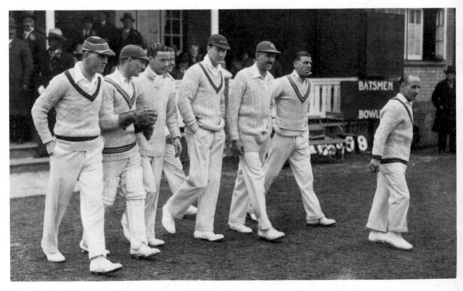

8. 'Tich' arranged many games in aid of Kent charities. Here he leads out his team to meet the West Indies at Gravesend, April 1933.

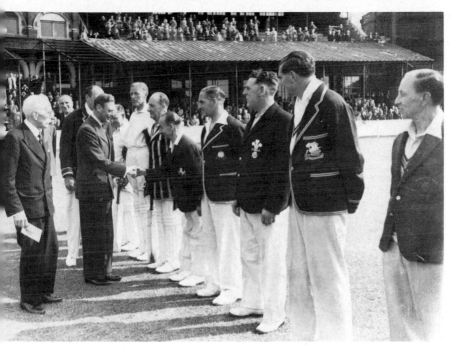

9. A day to remember, 23 May 1946. 'Tich' is presented to King George VI at The Oval before Old England v. Surrey.

10. Old England take the field. Left to right: Andy Sandham, Patsy Hendren, 'Tich', Maurice Tate, Maurice Allom and Percy Fender.

11. B. J. T. Bosanquet

12. D. W. Carr

13. Clarrie Grimmett

14. Richard Tyldesley

**EIGHT IMPORTANT FIGURES IN THE
HISTORY OF LEG-BREAK BOWLING**

15. R. W. V. Robins

16. I. A. R. Peebles

17. Richie Benaud

18. Robin Hobbs –
last of the line?

19. The Kent side in Freeman's last season, 1936.
Back row: Lewis, Ashdown, W. H. V. Levett, Watt, Fagg,
Wright
Sitting: Freeman, I. Akers-Douglas, B. H. Valentine,
Woolley, Todd

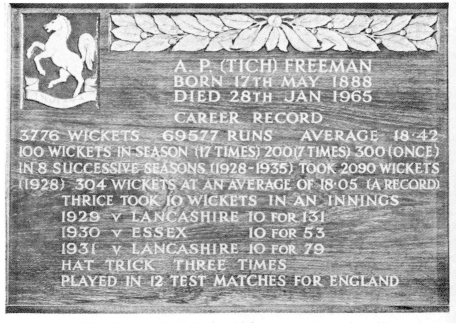

A. P. (TICH) FREEMAN
BORN 17TH MAY 1888
DIED 28TH JAN 1965
CAREER RECORD
3776 WICKETS 69577 RUNS AVERAGE 18·42
100 WICKETS IN SEASON (17 TIMES) 200 (7 TIMES) 300 (ONCE)
IN 8 SUCCESSIVE SEASONS (1928-1935) TOOK 2090 WICKETS
(1928) 304 WICKETS AT AN AVERAGE OF 18·05 (A RECORD)
THRICE TOOK 10 WICKETS IN AN INNINGS
1929 v LANCASHIRE 10 FOR 131
1930 v ESSEX 10 FOR 53
1931 v LANCASHIRE 10 FOR 79
HAT TRICK THREE TIMES
PLAYED IN 12 TEST MATCHES FOR ENGLAND

20. The plaque at Canterbury which commemorates the achievements of the greatest wicket-taker in the history of county
cricket.

7

Spinner Supreme, 1925–28

Gilligan returned home to a hero's welcome, but never again to play Test cricket although his energy, enthusiasm and good humour were to grace the game in other capacities for many more years. The career of Johnny Douglas was nearing its sad end and the incarnation of beauty, Frank Woolley, had toured Australia for the last time. 'Tich' got back to the business of carrying the Kent bowling upon his own shoulders and in the next three years was to take 507 wickets.

He had obviously enjoyed his batting exploits in Australia for he continued them into the English summer of 1925. At Old Trafford he hit his maiden fifty in first-class cricket in England. On the last morning he and Collins added 92 for the ninth wicket in 70 minutes and 'Tich' hit 66 of them, including nine fours. He was finally bowled by McDonald. At Tunbridge Wells, when Chapman made his debut in the county championship, Kent were beaten by Notts in a thrilling game; in the end Notts finished one place above Kent who were fifth in the table. Kent looked likely to accomplish the incredible task of scoring 384 in their second innings to win the match, for Woolley was at his most majestic. 'Tich' hit two sixes in his 41 not out, but he ran Frank Woolley out and Kent lost by 46 runs.

He played in no representative matches that season and his 146 wickets were all taken for Kent. When the county went on its customary tour of Scotland at the end of the season he once more caused havoc among the batsmen from north of the border. He had 9 for 43 against West of Scotland and then came a 12-a-side game against Berwickshire and District at Berwick. Freeman did not bowl in the first innings when the home side made 110; in the second, Collins took the first wicket and then 'Tich' took the next ten in 12 overs for 34 runs. Top scorer for the Berwick side was Lord Dunglass, better known as Sir Alec Douglas-Home; he was lbw to Freeman for 21.

With respect to the former Prime Minister, there was more serious work ahead for 1926 saw the arrival of the Australians and the National Strike which caused the abandonment of Kent's game with Oxford University. In fact, Freeman was to have no part in England's regaining of the Ashes. He was not selected for the Players, nor for the Test trial, nor for the Rest of England against the Champion County. Hearne played in the rain-ruined first Test and Stevens was recalled for the last two Tests. Stevens took 51 wickets at over 31 runs each during the season. The argument for Stevens' inclusion was always his all-round ability, but he accomplished little with the bat in Test cricket. Freeman meanwhile had 6 for 133 and 2 for 32 for Kent against the Australians at the end of August and, in all matches, took 180 wickets. This total was bettered only by Gloucestershire's Parker, another fine player consistently ignored by the selectors.

For Kent it was quite a memorable season; they finished third and made the largest profit, over £3,000, that they were to make in the years between the two wars. A young man named Les Ames played two games in the first team. He was in the side for the week at Tunbridge Wells and in the first game, against Warwickshire, although he did not keep wicket, he took four catches in the match. Two of them, Bates and Santall, were off 'Tich's' bowling, one in the deep and one at short leg.

There is a mistaken belief among many county cricketers today that 'Tich' only got the number of wickets he did because batsmen in his day were stumped or caught at long-on trying to hit sixes. This, of course, is very far from the truth. Frank Woolley took at least one catch off Freeman's bowling every season of the little man's career and in 1935, Woolley held 22 catches at slip off his bowling. Whatever the wicket, Freeman bowled to a slip and a forward short leg. If the wicket gave any assistance, he would bring in a silly point, a silly mid-off and a backward short leg. Frequently he bowled to five men clustered round the bat and the wicket-keeper crouched over the stumps.

A batsman might try to take the attack to 'Tich', but only two, Duleepsinhji and Jack O'Connor, managed it consistently without great mishap. For many, survival was the first consideration and few managed this with any sense of regularity. There were three or four known hitters for whom, as C. S. Marriott tells, both he and 'Tich' placed a man on the boundary for a familiar shot. 'No question of subtlety was involved; these were batsmen who were going to have their bash at that point, deep field or no, their main idea being to hit us clean out of the ground. It was good fun, a gay life while it lasted, but mostly a short one.'

The 484 stumpings that were made off 'Tich's' bowling were not all batsmen charging headlong down the wicket and swinging wildly, but mostly men lulled with subtlety to destruction. To stand any chance of competing with 'Tich' on equal terms a batsman had to use his feet, which is why many feel that 'Tich' would have had even greater success today, when batsmen with nimble footwork are a rarity, than he had in his own time.

Les Ames tells of a typical stumping off Freeman's bowling. In a Kent and Glamorgan game the Welshmen were not doing so well and Buckfield played 'Tich' with the utmost caution. He received two well-flighted leg-breaks of good length which he went forward to and met in the middle of the bat. The next delivery seemed exactly the same and Buckfield played the same shot, but the ball was just that little bit shorter and it was spun a little more so that it passed the outside edge and left the batsman stranded and off balance.

The season 1926 ended on a triumphant note at Northampton

where 'Tich' and Hubble added 93 for the eighth wicket to enable Kent to reach 233. He then dismissed Bellamy, but before he took his second wicket he had conceded 42 runs. He finished with 7 for 49, having taken 6 wickets for 7 runs in 56 deliveries. Woolley hit 217 in the second innings and when Northants set out on their forbidding task of scoring 499 to win Mr J. M. Fitzroy twice hit 'Tich' out of the ground, but the googly bowler got him in the end and finished with 5 for 82 to celebrate a fine season.

It was however, two other Kent players who stole the headlines that season. Percy Chapman, not yet captain of Kent, for whom he played only nine matches in 1926, led England to victory at The Oval so that the Ashes were regained and he became a national hero. Less of a hero to the public, but a hero to every professional cricketer, was James Seymour who retired from first-class cricket after 24 years of faithful service to Kent. Seymour received a demand for income tax on that part of his benefit money which accrued from entry fees paid at the gate. The Income Tax Commissioners, to whom he appealed, decided in his favour. The Crown took the case to the High Court where the decision of the Commissioners, was upheld. The Crown then appealed to the Court of Appeal and won. Ultimately, Seymour appealed to the Lords and won his case. Three years later, 'Tich' was to be very grateful for the efforts of James Seymour.

Hubble and Collins were two other players who were told that their services might not be required regularly during the 1927 season and in that year a new Kent side began to emerge. Todd, Brian Valentine and Crawley all played their first games for the county in 1927 and Les Ames became the wicket-keeper.

It is hard for us to realise now that it was only the persuasion of the exuberant Gerry Weigall that made Ames take up wicket-keeping. Of those who have kept wicket for England he alone would have been picked for his batting. Perhaps the only one to rival him in this connection was Jim Parks, but the Sussex player was a wicket-keeper of very modest accomplishment whereas Ames became one of the very best that the world has known. As well as being a great Test cricketer, Les Ames was to become one of the game's finest administrators and one who, through his judgement and integrity, was to help raise the status of the professional cricketer. He was the first professional cricketer to become a Test selector when he joined Brian Sellers, Tom Pearce and Bob Wyatt on the committee in 1949. Wyatt, a man who does not lavish praise easily, says of Ames that he is a very good judge of the game, with an extraordinarily wide experience.

One mentions this because Ames is as adamant today as he was when asked by *The Cricketer* nearly 30 years ago to select his best-ever England XI that Alf Freeman was the best spin bowler he ever saw. Laker he rates very highly. Benaud was a good bowler. Grimmett and O'Reilly were great bowlers. But Alf, in Ames' view, was the best of them all.

It is interesting to note, too, that Herbert Sutcliffe in his 'unghosted' book, *For England and Yorkshire*, published in 1935, puts 'Tich' first among spinners. Sutcliffe was doubtful as to whether Freeman had had a fair chance in Test cricket and makes the contrast with Wally Hammond who had failed in five Tests in a row and yet remained undoubted as England's leading batsman: 'Freeman has played so rarely in Test cricket that it is not possible fairly to give reasonable opinion on his qualifications for Test cricket. Judged by his record in county cricket in this country he takes more wickets season by season than any other bowler – and with recollection of the success that has attended Australian bowlers of a similar type when they have visited this country, one is bound to say that Freeman ought to have been a valuable man for England all the time he has been such a valuable man for Kent.'

The first batsman in first-class cricket to be stumped Ames, bowled Freeman was Mr J. B. Higgins of Worcestershire who was one of 'Tich's' five victims in the opening innings of the season at Folkestone, the first county fixture to be played there. Over the next nine years there were to be 258 other batsmen dismissed as Mr Higgins was that day.

Les Ames says that in that first game 'Tich' gave him a pre-arranged signal when he was about to bowl his googly, but thereafter he gave no signs and Les had to read what was coming even if

71

the batsman could not. He insists that Freeman's greatness lay not only in his command over length and the subtleties of flight, but in his ability to impart just the right amount of spin on the ball to beat the bat by a fraction of an inch or to clip the edge to give wicket-keeper or slip a catch. Others have turned the ball more, but none has turned it to such effect, nor given the impression that they were able to control the amount of turn as 'Tich' did.

The googly was used sparingly against the better batsmen, but it was well disguised and was instant death to the novice amateur. Les Ames tells how when 'Tich' spotted a new and colourful cap on the head of a young man he would hitch up his trousers with his forearms in the manner characteristically his own and you would know immediately that here was another victim. Two leg-breaks would be played solidly and they would not be turned sufficiently to worry the young man. Then suddenly would come a vicious googly and the young man was on his way back to the pavilion.

The top-spinner was 'Tich's' most potent weapon against the top batsmen, but the googly was always effective against the left-hander and was used with a sense of dramatic timing, never better exemplified than in that season of 1927. It was the first week of August, Canterbury week. Kent were playing Hampshire in the traditional fixture and had a marvellous opening day on the Saturday when they made 407 in 5½ hours before Wright, who gave Freeman excellent support that year, dismissed both openers, Brown and Brutton, for two runs. On the Monday Freeman was irresistible and took 6 for 38 as Hampshire were routed for 81. It then rained and no more play was possible until the last morning. Following on, Hampshire lost three wickets for 62, but the great Philip Mead then played one of his typically resolute knocks and held Kent at bay. He passed his hundred and Hampshire looked to have saved the game. All the time Mead was batting 'Tich' had not bowled him a googly and Les Ames, behind the stumps, could not understand why. The last over of the match began. Nine Hampshire wickets down. Freeman to Mead. The left-hander pushed forward with his 'they shall not pass' determination, but it was the googly and he was taken at slip by Woolley. Kent had won by an innings. Freeman's figures for the innings were 8 for 91, giving him match figures of 14 for 129. In the second match of Canterbury week he took 11 Notts wickets for 91 runs – 25 for 220 in the week!

It was one of the highlights of a splendid year. He finished sixth in the first-class bowling averages and took 181 wickets. Parker took 12 more wickets than 'Tich', but he bowled over 500 overs more. His talent was recognised outside the county, too: although the touring New Zealanders did not play Test matches, three Test trials were arranged and 'Tich' played in each of these. The first trial was ruined by rain. At Sheffield the North played the South and Holmes and Sutcliffe opened with an unbeaten stand of 269 so that 'Tich' was one of nine bowlers who failed to take a wicket. He was more successful at Bristol where, playing for England, he took the wickets of Hendren, Geary, Sibbles and Clark, nos. 4, 9, 10, and 11 in the Rest side, for 47 runs, before the rains came. Rain again interfered in the trial at Lord's in August, but this time he had an impressive haul – Bowley, Leyland, Bates and Ames, on trial in his first season, for 74 runs.

There was no argument now about the man's ability. *Wisden* was unequivocal in its assessment: 'Week in and week out he was incomparably the best bowler of his class in the country. Not only did he maintain a much better length than in the previous summer, but he made the ball do its work more quickly, and consequently proved more difficult . . . It was in no way surprising that he should have been asked to make one of the team to visit South Africa during the winter.'

So Freeman was back in contention for a Test place, but it was a strange team that he accompanied to South Africa. Chapman, Hobbs, Tate, Larwood, Duckworth, Jardine, Hendren and Woolley were all missing from the party; in fact, Woolley was to miss his first Test since that at The Oval in 1909.

It was originally intended that the side should be led by G. R. Jackson, the Derbyshire skipper, but illness forced him to withdraw and the side was led by Captain R. T. Stanyforth, a wicket-keeper whose three games for Yorkshire were to be played on his return from South Africa. Stanyforth's cricket had been played for the Army and, like his captain, Ian Peebles was to appear in Test cricket before he played for a county. Peebles was a mystery leg-break and googly bowler in the Carr tradition. A charming and witty man, he was to be preferred to Freeman within the next three years and so excite much controversy. Stevens was the third googly bowler in the party of 15 which was completed by E. W. Dawson of Leicestershire, G. B. Legge, the Kent amateur, R. E. S. Wyatt, Ernest Tyldesley, Sutcliffe, Holmes, the Leicestershire pair of Geary and Astill, Sam Staples of Notts, Elliott, the Derbyshire wicket-keeper, and Wally Hammond who was to begin his illustrious Test career in this series.

In truth, the South Africans were underestimated. They were to draw this series after being 2−0 down and were to beat England in the next home series and then in England in 1935. At the time of the MCC tour in 1927−29, South African wickets were still matting and of no great help to a bowler.

'Tich' began the tour in fine style when he bowled 18 overs against Western Province and took 5 for 15; only six wickets fell before rain halted the match. There was a highly impressive performance by a leg-break bowler on the other side, for 18-year-old H. G. Owen-Smith dismissed Tyldesley, Wyatt, Hammond and Stanyforth at a personal cost of 53 runs. Peebles and Stevens were in the MCC side so that over half the overs in the restricted game were bowled by leg-break bowlers − but then this was nothing unusual at that time.

Peebles had splendid success against Orange Free State and he bowled well against Transvaal. He won the vote over 'Tich' for the first Test in which Stevens also played. Stevens took three first-innings wickets, but it was the medium-pace bowling of Geary and Hammond which proved most effective. Sadly, Geary was to break down after the second Test and could not play again until the final match of the tour. In the first Test Sutcliffe and Tyldesley hit centuries and Hammond hit fifty, but no one else reached double figures. Nevertheless, England won by ten wickets.

All three leg-spinners were included for the second Test, Freeman replacing G. B. Legge. Deane won the toss and asked England to bat, and his decision seemed correct when the tourists were dismissed for 133. South Africa gained a first-innings lead of 117 which but for 'Tich' would have been larger. He dismissed both openers, Taylor and Commaile, Morkel and Palm in a spell of 29 overs which cost him 58 runs. England batted with much greater assurance in their second innings and left South Africa 312 to win. They never looked likely to make the runs and 'Tich' tore the heart out of the middle when he had Palm, Deane and Vincent all taken at slip by Wally Hammond in quick succession.

He routed Border by taking 8 for 48 just before the third Test, so enabling MCC to win in two days, and he retained his place for the rest of the series.

The third Test was drawn and 'Tich' took four wickets. England needed only to draw the fourth Test to win the series and, conscious of this fact and unwilling to give them the opportunity of playing safe, Deane again asked England to bat when he won the toss. England were bowled out for 265 and when South Africa batted Captain Stanyforth showed his inexperience by over-bowling Hammond and Staples after Hammond had had considerable early success, 'Tich' bowled only three overs, being called upon ultimately to break a ninth-wicket stand of 46 between Vincent and Bissett. South Africa led by 63 on the first innings. In their second knock England made only 215, so leaving South Africa the comparatively easy task of 153 needed for victory. Shortly after the start of the South African second innings Captain Stanyforth was hit under the right eye and forced to retire for the day. Incredibly, Freeman did not bowl but kept wicket in his absence. Stanyforth returned the next day and 'Tich' bowled Duminy, but South Africa won by four wickets.

For the fifth consecutive time Deane won the toss and, as in the fourth Test and for the same reasons, he invited England to bat first in the final Test. Holmes, who bagged a 'pair', fell immediately and from that point the home side played with such enthusiasm and inspiration that victory always seemed assured, even though they had lost the first day's play to rain. Stanyforth was absent from the England side, Stevens taking over the captaincy and Elliott coming in as wicket-keeper. Dawson came in for Peebles, but once more England batted without great conviction. They made 282 and South Africa gained a lead of 50, thanks almost entirely to a fifth-wicket stand of 136 in an hour and a half between Catterall and Cameron. Cameron, an effervescent and kindly man and a courtly wicket-keeper devoid of histrionics, hit 'Tich' for three fours and a six off successive deliveries. In the end he provided 'Tich' with his only wicket of the match. England subsided for 118 and South Africa won by eight wickets to draw the series.

Geary's 12 wickets at 15 runs each placed him top of the Test averages. 'Tich' had taken 14 wickets at 28.50. Hammond and Staples had each taken one more wicket than Freeman, but they had bowled 30 and 60 overs respectively more than he had. Neither Peebles nor Stevens had met with much success. In all first-class matches Freeman was the leading wicket taker. He returned to England with his reputation as a Test player enhanced and looking forward to the English season. The year was 1928.

8

Annus Mirabilis, 1928

Like wine, cricket has years which produce a special vintage. There are many of us who still savour the taste of 1947, that golden year when Edrich and Compton produced batting of full body and delicate bouquet. There are others who, if given the choice, would ask to enjoy again the flavours of 1928.

The season began damply, but after May the sun shone, the gods of cricket smiled and joy was abroad in the land. In 72 matches more than 1000 were scored and 37 times a side reached 500. Ernest Tyldesley, Sutcliffe, Mead, Hendren and Woolley all passed 3000 runs; 14 others reached 2000. Douglas Jardine made only 1133, but averaged 87.15 and beat 'the Master', Jack Hobbs, into second place. There were 414 centuries hit during the season.

Leslie Ames caught 69 and stumped 52 batsmen in his second full season of first-class cricket and was named as one of *Wisden*'s Five Cricketers of the Year – Duckworth, Leyland, Staples and J. C. White were the other four. It is strange to read now that *Wisden*'s one concern about him was that in taking the bowling of A. P. Freeman as well as he did, he had, however, been denied 'the practice of some other wicket-keepers in standing back to fast bowling'. Ruefully, we consider now that so many wicket-keepers

77

spend so much of their time standing back that wicket-keeping in general and stumping in particular have become lost arts.

The veteran S. F. Barnes reappeared at the top of the first-class bowling averages, having taken 20 wickets, 12 of them for Wales against the West Indies. Larwood, McDonald, Tate and Jupp enjoyed fine seasons. The name of Bowes was seen for the first time and Rhodes still took 100 wickets. The leg-break and googly bowlers thrived. Richard Tyldesley took 104 wickets and Lancashire won the County Championship. Ian Peebles played more first-class cricket. Percy Fender reached his 100 wickets and a young man named Walter Robins excited with 90 wickets and some spectacular batting.

On 27 July Alfred Percy Freeman reached 200 wickets for the season, and on 15 September he became the first, and one would conjecture the last, bowler to take 300 wickets in a first-class season. Considered in the context of 1928, his achievement was remarkable; today, when on average two or three bowlers a year reach the 100 mark, it seems miraculous. Yet, in the half-century that has elapsed since then, it has been fashionable to attempt to diminish the magnitude of the accomplishment.

First there was the suggestion that he dismissed mainly the 'rabbits', a theory touched upon earlier when quoting Cecil Parkin. Let us examine this charge. Those who have studied cricket of the 'twenties and 'thirties, and those who played the game then, are unanimous in their judgements of the general batting strengths of the counties then as compared with today: it is generally asserted that the first five or six batsmen were of a higher quality than their counterparts today, whereas the last three or four batsmen were definitely inferior to those who bat in those positions in our own times. An examination of the Kent scorebook of 1928 reveals that over one-half of Freeman's 246 victims for the county that season came from the first six in the batting order, and that only 12 of his wickets were no. 11 in the batting order. 45 of his victims were opening batsmen, but no. 5 was the man who fell to him most often. Among those who fell to him in county cricket were Gunn, Brown of Hampshire, Hobbs, Sutcliffe,

Hallows, Sandham, Whysall, Ducat, Ernest Tyldesley, Hammond, A. W. Carr, O'Connor, Wyatt, Mead, Worthington, Les Berry, the Nawab of Pataudi, Parsons, Iddon, Hopwood, Douglas, Fender and Charlie Barnett. No 'rabbits' in that list.

The second charge is that he was expensive in that he frequently conceded runs before he took the wickets of batsmen who had become satiated. It is conjectured that often his fives for 80 had started out as noughts for 50 or 60. This is an interesting argument and deserves close scrutiny. Until Marriott joined the side in the school holidays Freeman was the Kent attack. Sometimes he would open the bowling, possibly bowling a couple of overs of away-swingers or, more often, rubbing the ball in the dirt and getting on with his job. This lack of support meant that he tended to bowl all the time (not that he minded that) and that in 1928 he bowled 1976.1 overs and conceded 5489 runs. Far from helping him to buy his wickets, however, the need for him to bowl so much worsened his final figures, increasing the cost of wickets which had been cheaply won.

This is the case even with regard to such excellent figures as the 6 for 52 he took in the first innings against Northants at Northampton. Wright and Ashdown opened the bowling and Freeman replaced Ashdown after that bowler had sent down six overs and the score was 25 for 1. 'Tich', as was customary, dropped on a length immediately and began with two maidens. A single came from his third over and then Claude Woolley, brother of Frank, hit him for four. His fifth over produced a single and he dismissed Bellamy with the first ball of his sixth over: 1 for 6. His second wicket came with the first ball of his twelfth over: 2 for 15. By the end of his seventeenth over he had 4 for 28, all four being leading batsmen in the Northants side. In his remaining seven overs he conceded 24 runs to the hitting of Thomas and Clark, both of whom fell victims eventually to the leg-break. There was almost a repeat performance in the second innings when 4 for 41 (the first four batsmen) was transformed into 7 for 116 by the late hitters.

Later in the month, against Somerset at Taunton, he was brought on to bowl after six overs had gone. Jack Lee went lbw to the top-spinner with the first ball of his second over. Hunt went in his ninth, J. C. White in the thirteenth and Mays and Earle in the eighteenth and twenty-first respectively: 5 for 45. He was bowled for another hour to concede 22 more runs as Gaskell and Greswell lashed about them.

More marked are his experiences against Hampshire at Dover at the end of June. He had taken 5 for 61 in the first innings and eventually Hampshire were set over 400 to win. Freeman was bowling after only four overs and Brown and Hosie were dismissed with successive balls in his third over. Mead, Kennedy and Tennyson followed in the next 18 overs to give him figures of 5 for 58. Walter Livesey and H. R. Sprinks, with nothing to lose, scythed joyfully for the last wicket as 'Tich' bowled on and on and 99 runs were added. Sprinks was finally stumped by Ames off 'Tich' and Kent won easily enough. The little man's figures were 7 for 138 in 34.3 overs, his six maidens had been bowled in his first 19 overs and his first two wickets, one of them a Test batsman, had cost him six runs – the complete reversal of the accepted legend.

Examples are numerous: 5 for 23 against Worcestershire became 6 for 63 and, finally, 6 for 85; 4 for 19 against Essex became 6 for 87; and there were similar instances in the games against the West Indies, Notts and Derbyshire. In short, had Kent had adequate support bowling for Alf Freeman and been able to rest him when necessary, his figures would have been even more impressive than they are, but he would have been less happy, for he lived when he bowled.

For Freeman 1928 was a season of continuous triumph when the most accomplished batsmen found him their most difficult adversary. At Folkestone, against Gloucestershire, who finished fifth in the Championship table, he conceded 12 runs in his first three overs and then dismissed Neale, Barnett, Hammond, Stephens and Mills to finish with 5 for 28 and send the visitors from 58 for 3 to 100 all out. No county was spared and with Woolley's batting at its elegant best and the youthful Ames bubbling behind the wicket and with a bat in his hand, Kent finished in second place. Indeed, they seemed to have the Championship within their grasp, but successive defeats by Lancashire, the champions, Surrey and Notts in late July cost them dearly. As *Wisden* expressed it, 'Kent owed most to Freeman, who, putting a rare amount of spin on the ball and flighting it cleverly, bowled with so much skill that he went from one triumph to another.'

Freeman's triumphs were not confined to his games with Kent. He was back in the Players' side for the match at Lord's. Scoring at 83 runs an hour, the Players reached 423 on the first day, but on a perfect wicket the Gentlemen were 16 for 0 at the close and there seemed little fear of them failing to avoid the follow-on. Like so many others in 1928 and the years that followed, however, the Gentlemen had no answer to Freeman, and they went down before him on the Thursday. M. D. Lyon, D. R. Jardine, R. E. S. Wyatt, A. P. F. Chapman, R. W. V. Robins and W. B. Franklin joined the ranks of those dismissed by him in that memorable summer. Jardine, Wyatt and Jupp followed in the second innings and the Players won by nine wickets. 'Tich' was in the Players' side at Folkestone, too, and bowled his team to an improbable victory with 6 for 73 in the second innings. In all, he was to play in twelve Gentlemen v. Players matches and take 82 wickets. This total has been bettered only by W. Lillywhite, Alfred Mynn, D. Buchanan, A. G. Steel, G. A. Lohmann and Alfred Shaw in the numerous matches in which they played in the early years of the fixture, and W. G. Grace (271 in 85 matches), Wilfred Rhodes (103 in 38 matches) and J. W. H. T. Douglas (90 in 30 matches) in more recently recorded times. Freeman's record is rather good for one who 'failed to grasp his opportunity' against the best opposition. He is also the only player since the first world war to have taken 13 wickets in one of these matches; this he accomplished at Lord's in 1929.

Freeman's place in the Test team was assured. At Lord's, on 23 June 1928, he played for England in a home Test for the first time. It was an historic occasion as it was the first Test match ever accorded to the West Indies. Hobbs was missing from the England

81

side, but Tyldesley scored a hundred and Hammond and Sutcliffe got into the forties. The England captain was Percy Chapman and he hit fifty; Douglas Jardine was making his Test debut. Constantine took four wickets and England scored 401, enough to bring them an innings victory against an enthusiastic but inexperienced side.

Larwood and Tate opened the bowling and Freeman came on as first change. The West Indies' main hopes rested on Constantine who had built himself a considerable reputation as a magnificent hitter of the ball. He played a couple of lusty blows, but the first ball he received from Freeman he hit straight up in the air to mid-on where Larwood took the catch. It was 'Tich's' first wicket in Test cricket in England. Griffith followed later, and Freeman and Jupp, who had bowled with success in the first innings, bowled West Indies out for 166 in the second innings to give England an innings victory. The pattern was repeated in the second and third Tests. The West Indies were technically unable to cope with bowling of this quality and character, nor could their bowlers contain a batting line-up which read Hobbs, Sutcliffe, Tyldesley, Hammond, Jardine and Chapman. Freeman was the outstanding bowler of the series and topped the England averages with 22 wickets at 13.72 apiece.

The West Indian side did have its successes; there was the sensational victory over Middlesex at Lord's, Constantine's match, and there was a comfortable win over Kent at Canterbury. West Indies scored 282 in their first innings and Kent dissolved before the West Indian pace-bowlers so that the tourists led by 155 runs. Freeman's tenacity then gave Kent hope of pulling off a surprise win. He came on after six overs had been bowled and took the first eight wickets to fall at a personal cost of 80 runs. He was defied by Martin, the opener, who batted for more than three hours for his 82 before falling to Wright. 'Tich' captured the last wicket to finish with 9 for 104, having bowled nearly 35 overs on the trot. Kent's batting again crumpled before Constantine, Griffith and Browne. J. L. Bryan, 95 not out, batted with aggression and courage but 'Tich', 22, was the only other batsman to reach double figures and the visitors gained a handsome victory.

When the County Championship fixtures were completed 'Tich' took further toll of the West Indians with 11 wickets for a strong England XI at Folkestone, and Tom Richardson's 43-year-old record of 290 wickets in a season was in sight. Freeman started the next game at Folkestone, Kent v. MCC, with 281 wickets. In the festival atmosphere the ball was flying in all directions, first from the bat of Frank Woolley, completing 3000 runs for the season, and then from R. H. Bettington and F. T. Mann. 'Tich' took some stick, but he came out with 6 for 147 in the first innings. MCC were left 289 to win in 3½ hours. Errol Holmes was 'Tich's' first victim in the second innings and, after a stand, Charles Russell also fell to him. Newman followed quickly to provide him with his two hundred and ninetieth wicket, but Mann and Bettington bludgeoned MCC closer to victory. A leg-break on Mann's off-stump, an edge and there is Frank Woolley swallowing the catch at slip to give the little man the record – how appropriate it should come this way. It was appropriate not only because so many of Alf Freeman's victims were dismissed in this way, but because it was customary for these two to come onto the field of play together when Kent were bowling. Invariably they were at the tail of the side, walking together, the long and the short of it.

There was one more game at Folkestone, Gentlemen v. Players, in which Freeman set up victory for his side with a magnificent spell of bowling in the second innings, six wickets for 73, and brought his total number of wickets to 298, so bringing the unthinkable target of 300 within his sights.

There was the final match of the season to be played, Lancashire, the Champion County, versus the Rest of England. Of all the fixtures that have been discontinued over the past three decades, this is the saddest loss. It used to be such a splendid climax to the season, often producing games of rare quality. In that other vintage year, 1947, the game between Middlesex and the Rest of England brought records to some and joys to all. The fixture of 1928 could compare with it in grandeur.

The Rest of England side comprised ten men who had been

selected to tour Australia in the coming winter, and Frank Woolley whose non-selection caused much heated argument for several years to come; one of the selectors, 'Plum' Warner, accepted it as a mistake some 20 years after the event. The match at Kennington Oval began on Friday 14 September on a perfect wicket. This was Lancashire's third successive appearance in the match as champions of England. They had lost in 1926 to the side which had regained the Ashes a week before (in the second innings of that match runs had come at the rate of 125 an hour), but had drawn the fixture in 1927. The Champion County had not been victorious in the fixture since Yorkshire's win in 1905.

Mr L. Green won the toss and Hallows and Makepeace opened the Lancashire innings. There was a solid start which was consolidated by Ernest Tyldesley. At tea Lancashire were 202 for 2. After tea Lancashire's good position was wrecked, mainly by a fine spell from Hammond, and only another 55 runs were added while five more wickets were lost. Mr Green was caught at slip by Frank Woolley off the bowling of Alf Freeman. On the Saturday, before a large crowd, the Lancashire innings closed for 296. Richard Tyldesley, by one of the great ironies of cricket, moved out to a leg-break, missed and was stumped Ames, bowled Freeman. It was the bowler's three-hundredth wicket of the season. We shall never see its like again.

The ball with which 'Tich' dismissed Tyldesley was mounted and presented to him. Today it is in the cabinet which represents the small but interesting museum in the pavilion at Canterbury. It was Les Ames who, as manager of Kent, worked hard to establish this museum. After his old friend's death Ames approached his widow, Ethel Freeman, and asked if she would give one of the great bowler's souvenirs to the collection. Ethel Freeman knew little of cricket, but she knew it had been her husband's over-riding passion. 'Take what you like, Les,' she said; and when Les Ames had made his choice, she said simply, 'Alf would have liked that.'

Today it stands somewhat unobtrusively in the cabinet. To one side of it is a ball presented by Albert Mynn's nephew, on the other side is a ball from Strudwick's benefit at The Oval when

Huish stumped nine and caught one. Stumped nine! That would be a season's achievement today. Freeman's ball is labelled simply, 'Ball with which A. P. (Tich) Freeman took his 300th wicket in the 1928 season, creating a world record.' It is inscribed:

R. TYLDESLEY st Ames b Freeman 13

Overs	Mds	Runs	Wkts	Average
1976.1	423	5489	304	18.95

A. P. Freeman
Rest of England
v
Champion County
15 September 1928
300th
WICKET

It is well to linger for a moment on monuments to bowlers; they are rare. Canterbury boasts its Woolley Stand and its Ames Stand, and it is soon to have its Cowdrey Stand, but bowlers are not so honoured. Theirs is to toil. The 'Bat and Ball', the public house opposite the St Lawrence ground at Canterbury, which has had much good cricket talk and witnessed many a pint supped in the anguish of defeat and the joy of victory, sports its pictures of Felix and Mynn and the team of 1886, and some moderns, but there is no picture of 'Tich' Freeman. 'After all,' as was once written of Bill O'Reilly, 'he was only a bowler.'

The three hundred and fourth wicket came in the second innings of the match from which we have digressed. After Lancashire had been dismissed Hobbs and Sutcliffe, on the eve of departure for Australia, warmed all English hearts with an exhilarating display. Hobbs treated McDonald without mercy, hooking him furiously and hitting him high over the slips. He scored 150, the one hundred and fifty-eighth century of his career, and his last fifty came in half an hour. Sutcliffe, too, hit a hundred and completed 3000 runs for the season. Then Hendren took up the attack. At one time he hit 50 in a quarter of an hour and was finally out for 174. In 100 minutes on the Monday, the final morning, 226 runs were scored, with Ames and Hendren the main savagers. Chapman declared at 603 for 8. It had been scored in 5¾ hours, an average of 105 runs an hour. This was the quality of batsmanship in 1928, the year that 'Tich' Freeman passed 300 wickets.

Lancashire needed 307 runs to avoid an innings defeat. Larwood and Tate had half the side out for 107, then Hopwood and Ernest Tyldesley added 70 in half an hour during the course of which Tyldesley passed 3000 runs for the season. With five wickets standing at tea, Lancashire looked as if they had saved the match, but after tea Freeman took four wickets and the Rest of England had won by an innings. One of the greatest of English cricket seasons was at an end.

By coincidence, the man who was opposed to 'Tich' when he first played for Kent 2nd XI, S. F. Barnes, was top of both the first-class and second-class bowling averages in this great year, probably a unique performance.

For the next seven years Alf Freeman was to rule supreme among English spinners, taking over 200 wickets each season and coming close again to capturing the magical 300. Yet the figure of 'Tich' Freeman himself, bowling off his five paces with his rotary action like a spring snapping, becomes almost hidden behind the statistics. The man's achievement was so monumental, the man himself so small in stature. If he tends to get lost behind his records, it is because he tended to hide his talent. There was no exuberance at his record-breaking; he took it as a natural part of what he was trying to do for Kent. In a sense he did not know what all the fuss was about. Yet from all those who were close to him he excites the same type of comment: 'He was a lovely little man'; 'He was the best I ever knew'; 'I loved the man'. These are fulsome praises for a man who was so reticent. He inspired affection for two reasons. The first was his unquenchable effort and optimism – there has been no greater trier in cricket. The second reason was his humility.

In every assessment of him, it is necessary to place the man in his time. He was born to an age when a man was of a class, when the servant knew his place and respected the master to whom, on occasions, he proffered advice. Freeman accepted his class and the position it placed him in with regard to authority. He was a professional cricketer and as such was paid to do the thing that gave him the greatest pleasure in life. Those in authority had his unquestioned allegiance, and they returned his loyalty with the greatest affection and admiration. 'Chapman loved him,' says one old cricketer who knew them both. His efforts inspired love and yet he was the quietest and most undemonstrative of men. The hitch of the trousers showed determination; the Napoleonic fold of the arms showed satisfaction.

The position of the professional cricketer has changed dramatically, and rightly, since Freeman's day. Les Ames tells how, in the 1930s, when he was the greatest wicket-keeper batsman the world had ever seen and currently in the England side, he arrived for a match at Lord's with his wife. He was stopped at the gate and asked for 1s 6d, admission fee for his wife. With justified indignation he refused to pay and swept into the ground. Later in the day he was summoned before the secretary of the MCC and given a dressing down, and he had to pay the 1s 6d before he left the room.

Such an incident is unthinkable today when the cricketer demands full payment and respect for his abilities. On the other hand, perhaps recent happenings have clouded the issue for the younger reader who is used to pictures of Tony Greig, semi-naked, advertising cricket gear, and the county cricketer's sponsored car; in Freeman's day there was no television coverage to excite commercial interests.

There have, of course, always been cricketers linked with advertising. There is a splendid late Victorian advertisement involving William Gunn, the famous Notts professional. 'When playing against Surrey we wired Gunn, asking him if he attributed his success as a cricketer to Harness' Electropathic Belt? His reply was YES!' One does not know what Gunn was paid, but Bill Andrews, that lovely man from Somerset, tells of a conversation with E. W. 'Nobby' Clark, the Northants and England bowler. Clark, who had appeared in a beer advertisement in the 1930s, was

87

asked by Bill what he thought of all the modern advertising that cricketers did and the large sums that they were paid.

'What did they pay you for that beer advert, Nobby?' asked Bill.

Clark smiled ruefully. 'They sent my wife a bottle of Guinness at Christmas.'

These were the days before agents.

Canterbury week, in Freeman's day, was an occasion. Indeed, cricket everywhere was an occasion; there are pictures of men hanging from telegraph poles to watch Kent v. Yorkshire at Tonbridge in 1932. Bare torsoes or even open-necked shirts were unthinkable. Best clothes were worn, with hats or caps. The colour came not from advertising hoardings but from ladies' finery. Thursday of Canterbury week was Ladies' Day. It still is, and button-holes are worn by some, but the great splendour and beauty have passed. It was before such an audience of men in best clothes and caps and ladies in fine dresses that 'Tich' performed.

Every county had its favourites. There was 'Patsy' Hendren at Lord's, the great Jack Hobbs at The Oval and the lion-hearted Maurice Tate at Hove. Kent had the elegant, the majestic, Frank Woolley — 'There was all summer in a stroke by Woolley and he batted as is sometimes shown in dreams,' wrote R. C. Robertson-Glasgow — and Kent had 'Tich'. Men win the affection or the notice of crowds in diverse ways. Keith Miller roused them, as did Greig. Trueman perpetrated ideas of class or national warfare. Those men were extroverts, seeking, even if unintentionally, the eye of publicity. 'Tich's' popularity had no such foundation. He won the love of Kent through endeavour. The audience could identify with him. If Woolley was like a Greek god on earth for a brief while, then Freeman was of the earth, of the people. By his every action, his hours of bowling, his quiet acceptance of success and disappointment, he touched a chord in the hearts of those who watched, for this was the common stuff of the human heart.

Their affection for him was founded on his closeness to them. They understood his endeavours for he expressed their corporate ambition and struggles in his bowling. It was once said that the craze which surrounded Bing Crosby's singing in the 'thirties was because he sang as every man thought he sang in his bath. 'Tich' elicited the same response: he was a little man but he scaled the heights.

In his private life, too, he was of the ordinary folk. The pay packet was for the wife who returned the pocket money that she could spare. Both physically and domestically Alf was dominated by his wife. Ethel ruled him, but he accepted this as a natural part of the system. He loved a drink with the lads, but not in her presence. He smoked Passing Clouds almost endlessly, but not when she was around; Ethel did not approve. Les Ames tells of slipping in to see him one evening to find him hunched over a frugal fire. A voice came from the hall, 'Alf, I'm just going down to the shops.' Immediately a packet of Passing Clouds was pulled from an inner pocket and 'Tich' had a crafty drag.

There was the occasion when 'Hopper' Levett, who always drove him to away matches when he could because he so liked the man, had taken 'Tich' to Lancashire and Yorkshire where Kent were on tour. On the way back they had a puncture. It took them some time to get the car moving again and they were not back in Kent until one in the morning. 'Tich' was in a terrible state and when Ethel stormed to the door Howard Levett knew why.

Les Ames had a similar experience some years later when, after much persuasion, he took 'Tich' to a Test match. He had been asking him to accompany him for some time and 'Tich' finally agreed. The game finished at 6.30 and Les Ames drove them both back to Maidstone. They arrived back at nine o'clock to find Ethel waiting on the doorstep. 'He's not going out with you again. Keeping him out all night drinking!'

In his playing days Ethel would be at the ground at home matches at the close of play in order to drive him home. Their social life was very limited, yet in no way was Alf anti-social. He loved the company of his team-mates, but he was no great talker or contributor to discussion.

Doug Wright recalls that, as a young player, the only advice that he received from Alf was 'Keep it up to the bat.' For a young bowler this was indeed sound advice but, as Doug Wright says, the hardest thing in the world is to be able to spin the ball and keep a length, even though 'Tich' seemed to find no difficulty in doing so.

Tom Spencer, who started as a young player with Kent just as Freeman's career was drawing to a close, tells how the severest reprimand he ever received from the great spinner came when 'Tich' sent him to field at what seemed to Tom a rather strange position half-way to the boundary at square leg. As youth sometimes will, Tom Spencer decided to adjust his own position to something he considered more sensible. Alf deliberately dropped the ball short to the batsman who had been showing no aggressive inclinations but who, falling for the bait, pulled the ball up in the air to where Tom Spencer should have been. Alf made no gesture at the missed chance, except for the inevitable hitch of the trousers, and at the end of the over, as they crossed, he simply said to Tom, 'Go where I put you, lad.'

'Father' Marriott joined 'Tich' in the Kent side in the school holidays – he was a teacher at Dulwich College – and leg-break bowling from each end was the county's attacking weapon. Marriott was fascinated to watch the great man's subtle schemes developing and as a bowler, he knew that a batsman was being lured to a sense of false security and thence to destruction. Like all who knew him, he adored 'Tich': 'Considering the small size of his hands and fingers, the amount of spin he could put on the ball was astonishing. That, coupled with the colossal burden of work that he bore, made his control of length equally notable. Of course he struck an occasional bad patch, when he sent down a few loose ones, or the luck turned against him with a hard-hitting batsman getting away with catches put on the floor or dropping just out of reach. Tich, however, had in abundance that most precious quality of the first-rate spin bowler: the guts and capacity to stand unshaken under punishment, no matter what blows adverse fortune struck. He would take his sweater with a philosophic shrug, and a glint in his eye which said more plainly than words, ''All right, enjoy yourselves – but I shall be back.'''

'He made up for his short stature with a wonderful gift of

deceptive flight. His arm was obviously perfectly built for the googly, combining enormous strength of sinew with unusual suppleness. As a result he could flick it right over the top of his delivery with scarcely any perceptible drop of the wrist and continually had batsmen playing for a non-existent leg-break. Like all the best bowlers of his kind, he never overdid the googly but used it with fine judgment, matching his method to the situation and in particular to the individual batsman. To a tough, familiar adversary he would bowl it sparingly, relying mainly on leg-break and top-spinner, with an occasional wrong 'un suddenly mixed in as a menacing reminder that nobody, if he could help it, was going to settle down to a comfortable life. The heat was properly turned on when he was attacking either a batsman who was shaky about spotting the googly or one whose footwork was slow. Then Tich would really mix them, until the victim scarcely knew if he were coming or going, and we knew that barring accidents the end was not far off. He was extremely clever at flighting the higher, slower ball. For those who ventured out to it and found to their dismay that they were not quite there, you can imagine Leslie Ames' tigerish grin of welcome as he neatly removed a bail at the speed of light. Or maybe they did get near enough to push it into one of Percy Chapman's enormous hands at silly mid-off. To a left-hander, naturally, Tich bowled plenty of googlies, sometimes three or four to the over.'

Off the field 'Tich' would return to his occasional surreptitious pint and his packet of Passing Clouds. Often, in the hotel during away matches, he would play Patience for hours, waiting for the morrow when he could walk onto the field again and once more become the spider, spinning the web for the destruction of the flies.

9

Test Reject, 1928-29

There had been some speculation as to who should captain the MCC side that went to Australia in 1928 intent on retaining the Ashes. The names of Douglas Jardine and John Cornish White were mentioned in the press, but eventually, and with great popular approval, Percy Chapman, who had led England in the historic Oval Test of 1926, was given the post.

Although there was unanimous approval for the choice of Chapman as captain, there were some disagreements with the selection of the side. The most notable absentee was Frank Woolley who could consider himself rather unfortunate to have scored 3000 runs in an English season and still find himself not selected for the tour; as we have already seen, his omission troubled at least one of the selectors for several years to come. It was noted, too, that although 17 players were chosen for a tour for the first time, Freeman was the only leg-break and googly bowler in the side, an ominous portent. As it transpired the seventeenth member of the party, Sam Staples, the Notts all-rounder, was troubled by a rheumatic complaint in his back as soon as he arrived in Australia and returned home without participating in a fixture.

It was one of the best of England teams to visit Australia, in spite of the absence of Woolley, and the full party was: A. P. F.

Chapman (Kent) captain; J. C. White (Somerset), vice-captain; D. R. Jardine (Surrey); J. B. Hobbs (Surrey); H. Sutcliffe (Yorkshire); E. Hendren (Middlesex); M. Tate (Sussex); W. Hammond (Gloucestershire); C. P. Mead (Hampshire); M. Leyland (Yorkshire); E. Tyldesley (Lancashire); G. Duckworth (Lancashire); G. Geary (Leicestershire); H. Larwood (Notts); S. Staples (Notts); and Freeman and Ames of Kent. It was to be Hobbs' fifth and last tour of Australia, and amid the euphoria of victory there were to be indications, too, that not only was Chapman's reign coming to an end but a new star was rising in Australian cricket who would more than compensate for the passing from the scene of Collins, Bardsley, Macartney, Arthur Richardson, Taylor, Mailey and, during the series, Gregory and Kelleway.

Perhaps one of the most interesting of selections in the MCC side was that of J. C. White, the Somerset farmer, as vice-captain. 'Farmer' White had first played for England in 1921 and last played for his country in 1930. He played in 15 Tests in all and took 49 wickets with his slow left-arm bowling. He was a Test selector in 1929—30 and it was remarkable that he and Freeman were the only front-line spinners in the 17-strong party. Much attention was given at the time, and in later reports of the tour, to the fact that the utmost care had been given in selecting the side from the point of view not only of cricketing ability but also of social harmony, and the side left a most favourable impression wherever it went, both on and off the field. Certainly 'Tich' Freeman would have fitted into this pattern, and it was probably a factor in the selection of White. As one former Test cricketer remarked, 'I liked and respected Jack White tremendously as a man, but I didn't think he was a very good spin-bowler.'

As he had become the first man in cricket history to take 300 wickets in a first-class season, there was no way that Freeman could have been left out of the party to tour Australia, but there are those who believe that there was never any intention of playing him in the Test matches. They point to the fact that four years later, public sentiment demanded the inclusion of Maurice Tate in Jardine's team, but that never at any time did the Sussex bowler figure in the plans for recapturing the Ashes. The argument is a strong one, for the composition of the party suggests that spin had little part to play in the tactics for retaining the Ashes in 1928–29. A major factor in this decision was, of course, the Australian wickets: they were like iron and a batsman had only to play straight in order to score runs. For many bowlers they were death, and only if a bowler was very quick was the contest between bat and ball in any way even. It should be noted, however, that 'Tich' spent most of his life bowling on the very best of wickets.

As was mentioned in connection with Freeman's previous tours, the hustle for a place in the team for the first Test is the most crucial part of the tour for most players, because anyone who fails to make the team for that first Test is in danger of being overlooked for the rest of the series. So it was in 1928–29: from the XI which played in the first Test, only one change was made for the second – Geary, fit again, replaced Mead. There were no changes for the third and fourth Tests and, in the fifth Test, Leyland and Tyldesley replaced Sutcliffe and Chapman, both of whom were unfit although Chapman in fact made himself twelfth man for the match. This meant that apart from Staples, who had returned to England, Ames and Freeman were the only men not to play in a Test match and Ames would probably have been selected for the final Test for his batting had he not broken a finger shortly before the match.

'Tich' had every cause to be aggrieved, although it would have been totally out of character for him to have shown the slightest dissension or disappointment. He was not in the side for the opening game in Perth where White bowled commendably to take 3 for 59 and George Geary had his nose broken when he was hit in the face batting during the second innings of the drawn match. 'Tich's' first appearance was at Adelaide in a game in which nearly 1400 runs were scored and only 24 wickets fell. Hammond, Chapman and Pritchard hit centuries and Victor Richardson hit 231. Grimmett took 6 for 109 in 27.3 overs, 'Tich' had 5 for 180 in 44 overs. At Melbourne he bowled only seven overs and then he was in the side at Sydney for the game against New South Wales. This was the first time that an English side was ever to encounter Donald George Bradman. 'The Boy from Bowral', as he was then described by the press, had a prodigious record in grade cricket and was being hailed as Australia's new champion. He was to play his first Test match during the coming series and make his mark, though not without initial mishaps.

Chapman won the toss against New South Wales, Jardine and Hendren hit centuries, Hammond hit 225 and the MCC total was 734 for 7 declared, which, with the exception of the England innings at The Oval in 1938, was the highest total through which Bradman was ever to field. New South Wales lost three quick wickets before Kippax and Bradman stopped the rot. They took the score from 52 to 142 before Kippax was out, and then Bradman and Kelleway put on 68. Bradman was 13 short of his century when he was out. *Wisden* wrote that he had 'survived two or three appeals for leg-before before Freeman, with whom he was never comfortable, bowled him round his legs.' So Alfred Percy Freeman added another achievement to his record, as the first English bowler to dismiss the Don. He finished with 5 for 136, but he did not take a wicket when New South Wales followed on and Kippax and Bradman scored centuries as the game drifted to a draw with Jardine, Hendren and Sutcliffe bowling.

There were two more matches before the first Test. The first was at Sydney against an Australian XI, the second was against Queensland, now a Sheffield Shield side, at Brisbane where the first Test was to be played. Both matches were won. White played in both matches, Freeman only in the second, which was finished in under three days. Hammond and Geary bowled 13 overs between them without success before handing over to Freeman and White. Queensland were dismissed for 116, Freeman taking 5 for 51. He took two more wickets in the second innings, so arriving at the eve of the first Test with 17 wickets from the six innings in which he had bowled. White had 18 wickets, having bowled in eight innings, and these two were the most successful of England's bowlers.

The selection committee for the tour (Chapman, White, Jardine,

Hobbs and Tyldesley) spent many hours on the night before the first Test debating the composition of the side and when it was announced it caused some concern among England supporters. In order to strengthen the batting, the England selectors had included Mead and settled for three front-line bowlers, Larwood, Tate and White, with support from Hammond who, after taking three wickets against Western Australia in the opening match of the tour, had taken only two wickets since. It was an incredible gamble, but fortune hangs on a thread. It had been generally expected that Geary and Freeman would be in the side for the first Test and, as *Wisden* said, Freeman 'had real excuse for feeling disappointment at not being included in the team at Brisbane'. Influenced by the thought of timelessness, the selectors erred on the side of caution. It was the first hint of a change in attitudes in Test cricket and although the leg-break bowler was to survive for many more years, it was the first toll of his death knell.

In the event, England scored 521 in their first innings thanks to a superb knock by 'Patsy' Hendren, most ably supported by Harold Larwood. Gregory broke down and limped out of Test cricket for ever. Kelleway was taken ill and he, too, passed from the scene. On top of this a series of missed chances aided England in their efforts.

When Australia batted they lost four wickets for 44 runs in just over an hour at the end of the day. Before a run had been scored Bill Woodfull was out to a catch by Chapman off Larwood's bowling which has been described by some as the greatest catch that even this great fielder ever took. In the gully he dived full length to hold the ball in his left hand, his arm fully extended. For S. J. Southerton, *Wisden*'s correspondent, it was the crucial point of the whole series.

The three quicker bowlers dismissed Australia for 122 – Larwood 6 for 32, Tate 3 for 50, Hammond 0 for 38, Gregory absent. England then scored 342 for 8 in their second innings, Clarrie Grimmett taking 6 for 131. Australia needed 742 to win. Ponsford was caught behind off Larwood and they were 17 for 1 when play ended early through bad light. During the night it rained heavily and the following morning the sun shone brightly. Australia were caught on a glue-pot. They were all out for 66, Gregory again absent. J. C. White took 4 for 7 in 6.3 overs. For the second time in a tour of Australia 'Tich' Freeman had been denied an opportunity to bowl on the type of wicket on which, in England, he had proved consistently devastating. His misfortune , and the faults in England's selection, were obscured by a victory which owed a good deal to luck but which, like any victory by 675 runs, ended all argument.

Freeman took 8 for 32 and 7 for 74 against a Combined Country XI at Warwick in the one game that separated first and second Tests, but there was no chance now that he could force his way into the side. He continued to do well in all the games in which he played, but he was not part of the plans in Test matches.

White had a good series and a good tour, and Grimmett, of course, was leading wicket-taker for Australia. Bradman was dropped for the second Test but returned to record the first of his Test centuries. The last Test, having gone on for eight days, was won in the end by Australia so that they saved themselves from complete disgrace, losing the series by four to one. Wally Hammond became the pride of England when he scored 905 runs in the series.

Perhaps we should pause and consider that last statistic because there are those who believe that Hammond's record and Bradman's breaking of it a year later marked the end of an old and noble spirit in cricket. This is in no way to point a finger of accusation at these two wonderful cricketers, and any who saw them bat will cherish the sight for as long as they live. Rather it was their imitators and followers in whom the spirit died and batsmanship gave way to run-accumulation. There was an inkling of this in the final Test of the 1928–29 series, when 'the cricket all through proved dreadfully slow' (*Wisden*) and which at that time was the longest in history, lasting into the eighth day. Geary bowled 81 overs in the first Australian innings and took 5 for 105. White bowled 75.3 overs and took 2 for 136. Cricket was moving out of the age that 'Tich' knew and was only ten years away from the timeless Test at Durban which ended in a draw after ten days.

It is only with the advantage of historical perspective that we can make these judgements. Few, if any, were conscious of them at the time. England had trounced Australia four Tests to one. Hammond had broken all records. The heroes came home in triumph.

'Tich' came home to Kent and his benefit year. He was 41 years old. For Kent it was an uneasy season and they dropped from second to eighth in the County Championship table. There was criticism of both captain and Committee of which the Committee showed an obvious awareness in the annual report. As bowlers, Marriott and Ashdown had indifferent seasons, but of one thing the Committee was sure. 'Freeman was as brilliant as in 1928, and may fairly to be said to have carried the side.' In all matches he took 267 wickets at 18.27 each. No other bowler in the country reached 200 wickets. Leg-spin bowling was, as ever, very much to the fore with T. B. Mitchell of Derbyshire establishing himself with 113 wickets and gaining a Test trial, and Richard Tyldesley, Walter Robins and Ian Peebles all passing the 100 mark.

'Tich' had the game with Gloucestershire at Canterbury for his benefit, but it was the first encounter with Gloucestershire that remains most vivid for Les Ames. Gloucestershire had started their season with four away games, two of which they had won. They returned to Bristol to entertain Kent in good heart. It was also the welcome home for the hero of England, Wally Hammond. A huge crowd arrived on the Saturday to see the great man and they did not have to wait long before he came to the wicket. Ashdown bowled seven economic overs and then Freeman was given the ball. He had immediate success as Sinfield went lbw to the top-spinner for 8 with the score at 18. Hammond came to the wicket with a tremendous roar echoing round the ground.

It was customary for 'Tich' to greet a new batsman with a googly, but on this occasion he beckoned to Les Ames as Wally Hammond, for whom they both had the greatest admiration, was walking to the wicket and said, 'Wally has a type of walking shot which he plays to the leg-break on a good wicket like this. He'll probably be expecting the googly, Les, so I'll give him the leg-break instead and you may have a chance.'

'Tich' bowled a ball well pitched up on the off stump and Wally did play his walking shot, but it turned away sharply. He missed it and Les Ames whipped off the bails. The ground was silent as the great batsman trudged back to the pavilion. 'Tich' had spoiled the party. It was, in fact, one of 54 dismissals that Les Ames made off 'Tich's' bowling that year, 36 of them stumpings.

There was no holding 'Tich' in that particular innings at Bristol, and on a fine wicket he took 7 for 50 to bowl Gloucestershire out for 119. Then he hit 45 not out, out of a ninth-wicket stand of 62, took four more wickets in the second innings, including both openers stumped by Ames, and Kent won by eight wickets on the Tuesday afternoon.

There were several memorable achievements by the little man that season, but it was at Maidstone in late July that he accomplished the one distinguished feat which had until then eluded him. It was, however, a match of mixed fortunes for Kent, who were leaders in the County Championship before the match began, and who lost the game by 189 runs and declined from that point in the season. Lancashire, the visitors, won the toss and batted on a good wicket. Wright, Ashdown, Woolley and Hardinge failed to make any impression on the batsman, but 'Tich' sent down 42 overs and took all ten wickets for 131 runs. He was to accomplish the feat twice more before the end of his career.

His benefit match with Gloucestershire at Canterbury was scheduled for the August Bank Holiday week-end. The weather was dull on the Saturday and there was no play whatsoever on the Tuesday, but over 20,000 people came to see the cricket and to say thank-you to the man who had become part of the folk legend of Kent cricket. He took four for 100 (for once Marriott had the better share of the wickets) and scored four before being caught at slip by Hammond off the bowling of Parker. The receipts from the drawn match were £1223 11s. There were subscriptions amounting to £377 5s and the collections at grounds raised £769 8s 11d. Interest on the deposit account was £11 1s 1d, and when expenses for stationery and printing had been deducted 'Tich' was left with £2381 6s 1d. These accounts show how much the organisation of benefits has changed over the years until they have now become complex and lucrative business ventures. Nevertheless, the benefit that 'Tich' received in 1929 was £500 greater than any other Kent benefit until that time and it was to remain a Kent record until after the second world war.

'Tich' ended Canterbury week with a wonderful performance against the champions to be, Notts. He opened the bowling with 'Father' Marriott in each innings, taking 8 for 74 in the first innings and 6 for 57 in the second. It is difficult to imagine where the fallacy that he was only effective against 'rabbits' ever originated, but as a corrective the next match was against Sussex at Hastings. 'Tich' took 9 for 237 in the match, but this was the first occasion that he really encountered the rapier bat of Duleepsinhji, who hit 115 and 246 in the match. Of all the batsmen to whom 'Tich' bowled, Duleepsinhji gave him the greatest problems. (The other to trouble him was, surprisingly, Jack O'Connor of Essex.) The nephew of the great Ranji was so quick on his feet and seemed to see the ball so much earlier than most that he constantly took the attack to 'Tich', dancing nimbly down the wicket to him and driving him with that exquisite grace which adorned cricket for all too brief a period.

'Tich' did not play for the Rest of England against Notts (neither did J. C. White who had had a good season) but in the Test trial he took five Rest wickets, Ames, Crawley, Killick, Robins and Wyatt, for 132. It was at Lord's in July, however, that he had one of his greatest triumphs. This was the match in which he took 13 of the Gentlemen's wickets.

The Gentlemen won the toss on a fine day and batted on a splendid wicket. Tate at once bowled Crawley and Hammond had Wyatt caught behind, but Killick had settled in well and he and Carr retrieved the position. With the score at 38 'Tich' was brought on to bowl, but without any immediate success. Carr and Killick had added 48 runs and the score was 66 when the Notts captain was suddenly unable to curb his natural instincts any longer. He jumped out to drive at Freeman, missed and was stumped by Duckworth. Having broken the partnership, 'Tich' routed the rest of the batting. B. H. Lyon went lbw and Percy Fender was bowled, both without scoring. The Gentlemen's middle order was composed of natural hitters who were ill-equipped to deal with Freeman at his best. He was bowling into a slight breeze, which was not what he generally preferred, but he flighted the ball cleverly and turned it sufficiently. Allen, Haig, Robins, Benson and, ultimately, Killick succumbed to him, Killick having scored 59 of the Gentlemen's 138 before edging a leg-break to Frank Woolley at slip. His runs came in an hour and a half out of the 83 scored while he was at the wicket. Freeman's final figures were 20.3–5–41–8.

Chapman had not returned to England after the tour of Australia so J. C. White captained England against South Africa. The South Africans were a young and somewhat inexperienced side and the England selectors adopted a rather ambivalent attitude towards them. Duleepsinhji played in the first Test, in which Killick also made his international debut, but did not play again for the rest of the series. Hobbs played only in the last Test. Jack O'Connor made his Test debut in the second match and then was jettisoned for the remainder of the series. 'Tich' was called in to save the day after things had not gone too well for England at the start.

Percy Fender was recalled to the England side for the first Test match, having shown fine all-round form in the county matches. The match was, in many senses, a continuation of the final Test against Australia a few months earlier. It took South Africa 7½ hours to reach 250 and gain a first-innings lead of five. Mitchell, making his Test debut, batted seven hours for 88, and in the entire match batted over 9½ hours for 149 runs. The match was drawn.

The second Test was also drawn. Walter Robins made his Test debut, replacing Fender as the leg-spinner. O'Connor, who also bowled leg-breaks, did not bowl on the occasion of his Test debut. Again South Africa led on the first innings, but Leyland and Tate hit centuries in the second innings and South Africa struggled in bad light to save the game. Cameron was knocked out by Larwood and shortly afterwards the match was abandoned.

The South Africans had been badly hit by illness and injury, but it was apparent that the England selectors, as on the previous tour of the Dominion by Captain Stanyforth's team, had grossly underestimated the strength of the opposition. There was disquiet among cricket followers and agitation before the third Test. 'The previous England teams not having given entire satisfaction, the younger element failing to rise to the occasion, the Selection Committee brought in Woolley, Bowley and Freeman for O'Connor, Killick and Robins. The changes were all to the good,' *Wisden* reported.

Robins had had match figures of 5 for 79 on his Test debut so could consider himself a little unlucky, but he had failed with the bat and was always picked for his all-round ability. Killick never played another Test. A batsman of quiet charm, he entered the ministry and died the true death of a cricketer when he collapsed at the wicket during a clergy match at Northampton. For South Africa, Cameron had not recovered from the effects of his knockout blow and Van der Merwe took over as wicket-keeper while J. P. Duminy, who was on business in Switzerland, was called in to complete the South African side whose ranks had been thinned by further injuries.

Deane won the toss and South Africa had first knock on the Leeds wicket against the bowling of Tate and Larwood. Siedle was bowled by Larwood with only one run on the board, but Catterall and Mitchell dug in and took the score to 75 before Mitchell was bowled by Tate. The third wicket did not fall until after lunch. Catterall had batted well and scored 74 out of 120 when he aimed a dreadful leg swipe at Freeman and was bowled. 'Tich' had conceded 34 runs before taking this wicket but now, in a two-hour period after lunch, he destroyed the South African batting. They collapsed to 170 for 8 and when Van der Merwe was caught at slip by Hammond off Freeman, they were 219 for 9. This was Freeman's fiftieth wicket in Test cricket, and he had reached the mark in his tenth Test match. It was to take Ian Botham exactly the same number of Tests to reach the same mark 49 years later, and Botham, who had some far easier pickings than 'Tich', was considered a wonder boy.

Vincent saved South Africa from complete humiliation with an innings of 60 in 70 minutes. He hit four sixes and six fours and took 47 of his runs off 'Tich' who finally bowled him, finishing with 7 for 115. England gained a lead of 102 on the first innings, then Owen-Smith, whose leg-breaks were used very sparingly in the series, hit a brilliant century in the South African second innings when Freeman had three more wickets. England were in some trouble at the start of their second innings, but Frank Woolley played quite beautifully and England took a lead in the series.

Carr took over the England captaincy from J. C. White for the fourth Test match and although South Africa fielded what, on paper, looked a stronger side than the one they had at Leeds, they were beaten by an innings and England won the series.

Injuries robbed England of Hammond, Tate and Larwood who were replaced by Wyatt, Geary and Barratt. England batted the whole of the first of the three days and scored 427 for 7. Wyatt and Woolley hit hundreds, Wyatt being the first amateur since the war to make a hundred in a Test match for England. On the Sunday it drizzled all day and play could not begin until after five past one on the Monday. Carr declared at the overnight score and after Barratt had dismissed Catterall, 'Tich' was soon in operation. South Africa were all out in just over three hours. They had no answer to the little spinner who took 7 for 71. South Africa followed on and were 15 for 3 before the close. They fared better on the last day, but once more there was no answer to Freeman. Though not too well supported in the field, he took 5 for 100 and England had won the rubber.

There were more changes in the England side for the last Test at The Oval, Hobbs, Hammond, Ames and Clark coming in for Bowley, Hendren, Duckworth and Barratt. Sutcliffe became the first batsman to score a century in each innings of a Test match twice, after Taylor and Deane had batted excitingly on a perfect wicket and raised South Africa from 20 for 3 to 234 before they were parted. England batted for the second time 234 in arrears, but saved the game with ease.

On a wicket which gave no help to the bowler, 'Tich', though sending down very few bad balls, had the most expensive analysis of his whole first-class career: 49−9−169−0. Although he was to remain the leading bowler in England for another six years, this, Les Ames' first Test match, was to be 'Tich' Freeman's last. Wilfred Rhodes, at the age of 52, was to play for England again, Greville Stevens was to bolster a poor Test record in the West Indies, Richard Tyldesley, with a far less impressive record than Freeman, had Test matches in front of him as did Peebles, Robins and Mitchell, but Test cricket had seen the last of Alfred Percy Freeman. In his last series he had been England's leading wicket-taker with 22 wickets at 24.86. Maurice Tate was the only other bowler on the England side to have taken ten wickets, and they had cost him 33.30 each.

10
Past Master,
1930–34

The selection committee for the Test series against Australia in
1930 consisted of Mr H. D. G. Leveson-Gower, the chairman,
who had just been made President of Surrey County Cricket Club,
Mr F. T. Mann, who had relinquished the captaincy of Middlesex
but still played occasionally, and Mr J. C. White, who was captain
of Somerset. Percy Chapman was appointed captain, but this time
he was to find himself in the same position as Carr had been in four
years previously; he was to be replaced for the final Test when Bob
Wyatt took over the captaincy. This was not a popular decision,
but then little that the selection committee did that summer was
popular, and much of it was incomprehensible. For example, for
the fifth Test they chose 13 players, two of whom were wicket-
keepers. Duckworth had kept wicket in the first four Tests, but
Ames was in the party for The Oval. In the event, Ames and
Parker were omitted on the morning of the match, but followers of
the game found it difficult to understand why two wicket-keepers
had been called up and why the decision as to who should occupy
this important post could not have been taken at the full selection
meeting earlier.

The other man omitted from that Test, Parker, was the second
leading wicket-taker in the country. He was 48 years old and had

played his one Test match in the horror year for English cricket, 1921. His omission from The Oval Test had a remarkable sequel for he took 10 for 126 in the match after the Test to give Gloucestershire a tie with the Australians at Bristol.

The problem for England was that although their batting was adequate, their bowling was never good enough to prevent Australia from making huge scores on perfect wickets. All the same, three of the first four places in the England bowling averages were filled by leg-break bowlers: Richard Tyldesley, 7 wickets at 33.42; R. W. V. Robins, 10 wickets at 33.80; and I. A. R. Peebles, 9 wickets at 39.33. Maurice Tate had 15 at 38.26 and Harold Larwood 4 at 73 runs each! Grimmett took 29 wickets for Australia and was the key factor in Australia recapturing the Ashes. Woodfull's opinion was that the Australians could have won without Bradman, but not without Grimmett.

This was, of course, the year in which Bradman first presented great problems to England's bowlers, scoring 974 runs in the series. 'All summer it has been agreed by cricketers of judgement,' wrote Cardus, 'that slow spin was the answer to Bradman.' And Ray Robinson: 'Bradman disliked playing forward in defence; usually he stood motionless as a statue until he learned the direction and length of the ball, then made all his movements in a flash. That is why, now and again, a flighted leg-break found Don with his mind not made up, and yielded a catch to slip or 'keeper'.'

The England side for the first Test included two leg-spinners, Tyldesley and Robins. England won by 93 runs and both bowlers returned good figures. For the second Test at Lord's J. C. White replaced Tyldesley and England were beaten by seven wickets. Tyldesley came back at the expense of Robins for the third Test and was the only spinner in the side apart from Leyland since White was also dropped. Australia scored 566 and the match was drawn. In the fourth Test two spinners, Peebles and Goddard, played. For the fifth Test Peebles had to rely on Leyland for his only spin support. Australia won by an innings and Peebles sent down 71 overs to take 6 for 204.

There were those who believed that Ian Peebles was Bradman's Achilles' heel. Certainly Bob Wyatt, captain in the last Test, was of this number. Peebles was indeed a very fine bowler and in his selection there were echoes of D. W. Carr, for Peebles' debut in first-class cricket had been in the Gentlemen and Players match at The Oval in 1927. As we have already seen, he had played Test cricket in South Africa at the age of 20 before he had become attached to Middlesex. The reasons for his selection in preference to Freeman are apparent. Once more it was the romantic amateur rather than the staid professional. The decision was not motivated by class considerations, but by the belief, however fallacious, that only the amateur had the spark, the sudden flash of inspiration uninhibited by professional restraint, that could produce the unplayable ball. Sadly, in Peebles' ascent there were already signs of his decline for, again like Carr before him, in experimenting with the googly he was frequently losing the ability to bowl the leg-break. In all, Peebles was to play 13 Test matches, one more than Freeman, and take 45 wickets, 21 fewer than the Kent man.

Peebles was to become one of the most sagacious and amusing writers on the game which to him was always just that – a game. He had no doubts as to his own ability compared to Freeman's. 'Tich Freeman was the best and most consistent of English tweakers,' he wrote. 'Looking back, it seems strange that Freeman never played against Australia in a Test match in this country.'

Had Ian Peebles ever entertained any doubts as to what the general public thought of him in comparison to 'Tich', his bank manager left him with no uncertainties. In his autobiography, *Spinner's Yarn*, a book as delightful as the man himself, he tells of his introduction to the person who was to become a life-long friend: 'One morning I walked round the corner from Lower Grosvenor Place, where I was living, and went into the first bank I came to, which happened to be Barclay's, Belgravia. On hearing that I wanted to open an account the clerk summoned the manager, a splendidly portly Pickwickian figure named Dickinson, with a florid complexion and G. K. Chesterton *pince-nez* askew on his nose. He enquired my name and on hearing it he looked at me

107

thoughtfully. "Do you play for Middlesex?" he asked. I said I did. "Well," he said, "'Tich' Freeman's a bloody sight better bowler than you'll ever be – hand over.'"

Robins, too, took a fair amount of criticism in the press as he had been picked ahead of 'Tich'. Robins was a fine fielder and a good bat, though not a particularly reliable one, and was to become an England captain and a Test selector. He was to play in 19 Test matches and yet finish with two wickets less than 'Tich' in his 12 Tests.

It all seems very strange from this distance. If spin was the answer to Bradman, why was 'Tich' never selected? On the eve of the series all the pressmen were confident that he would be a trump card against Australia in England. 'What a rod in pickle for Australia this summer!' wrote Frank Thorogood. And a year later he wrote, as editor of the *News Chronicle Cricket Annual*, 'When in 1928–29 England kept the Ashes down under without employing Freeman, who was a member of the MCC party, the omission was probably more significant of the weakness of Australia at that period than of any slight to the famous Kent bowler. Again last year he took no part in the Test matches, although losing nothing of his wonderful form, and many good judges still think that a grave mistake was made.'

Neville Cardus, by 1930 already feeling that the best was behind him and few were prepared to work at the game as of yore, stated emphatically that the school of the googly was on the wane for the bowling of it demanded an exacting discipline which was beyond the contemporary cricketer who sought a cheaper market. 'The googly,' he insisted, 'can be mastered only by long labour and much philosophy. As I write, there is only one authentic googly bowler playing – his name Freeman.' Freeman's only games against Australia had been in Australia in 1924–25 and since then he had become the complete master of his art and broken all records. Grimmett and Mailey were both far more successful bowlers in English conditions than they were in Australia. Bradman himself paid tribute to Freeman as a fine bowler in England.

If one has seemed to protest too much at the way in which Freeman was ignored by the selectors in 1930, it is because the evidence for his inclusion was as great as his omission was bewildering. In all matches in 1930 he took 275 wickets at 16.84 runs each. Parker was next with 179 wickets. The leg-break bowlers in the Test trial were Robins, who took 53 wickets at 22.54 in the season and G. T. S. Stevens, who took 25 wickets at 31.08 but was still looked on hopefully as a messiah in appearances which were becoming less and less frequent.

The Test trial was played on the last day of May and on 2 and 3 June. At this time Freeman was beginning a phenomenal spell of bowling. In five Championship matches, against Essex, Hampshire, Gloucestershire, Derbyshire and Warwickshire, he took a total of 64 wickets for 664 runs. Tom Pearce, Russell, Cutmore, Townsend, Wyatt, Worthington, Santall, Dacre, Barnett, Arnold, Mead and Tennyson were among the 'flies'. Tom Pearce says that he never could read 'Tich'. He just used to play forward and hope for the best. More often than not, he was lucky enough to get an edge that would send the ball skidding off to the third-man boundary. 'Tich' did not like it, but he just used to hitch up his trousers and try again and Tom Pearce, ever the chivalrous gentleman, gives him best.

On Saturday 14 June, at Tonbridge, when he took eight Derbyshire wickets for 70, he became the first bowler to reach 100 wickets in the season and only J. T. Hearne, on 12 June 1896, had reached that total earlier in the season. From 21 May to 20 June, in nine matches, 'Tich' took 104 wickets and it is doubtful whether any bowler has ever taken 100 wickets in a month. In the month of June itself he took 91 wickets.

This was not the end of his triumphs. On 6 August he reached 200 wickets for the season and a week later Kent visited Southend for the game with Essex. Kent finished fifth in the championship, although only Gloucestershire in second place won more games. Essex finished one place lower than Kent so the contest was expected to be a keen one. On the Wednesday, Kent were dismissed by Nichols and Ken Farnes, then an unknown from Royal

Liberty Grammar School, Romford, for 122. Essex passed the Kent total with only three men out, all to Freeman, but then collapsed as the little man took complete command. He had come into the attack after Ashdown had bowled nine overs and from that point bowled without a break. In 30.4 overs he took all ten wickets at a cost of 53 runs. This was the second year in succession in which he had taken all ten wickets and, in so doing, he became only the second man in cricket history to perform the feat twice; the first had been V. E. Walker of Middlesex in 1865.

After the Test matches were over, the Australians came to Canterbury straight from the tied match with Gloucestershire at Bristol. Their match with Kent began on Wednesday 27 August, Don Bradman's twenty-second birthday. The St Lawrence ground was flooded with birthday greetings and the sun shone. Australia won the toss and Woodfull and Ponsford opened before a crowd of 13,000. Woodfull was run out and Ponsford fell to 'Tich'. The great Don was sorely troubled by the mixture of leg-breaks, googlies and top-spinners that he received from 'Tich' and shortly before lunch there was a raucous appeal for lbw. Up went 'Sailor' Young's finger and the Don was out for 18. The Kent crowd saluted its own hero. He responded by adding the wickets of Jackson, Fairfax and Walker, finishing with 5 for 78. Kent gained a lead of 46 on the first innings, and when Australia batted again Ponsford fell to Ashdown and Woodfull was lbw to Freeman. Bradman had been in for only a few minutes when he went back to Freeman, was beaten and hit on the pad. Another strident appeal rent the heavens, but this time 'Sailor' Young's finger stayed down. It must have been the very closest of decisions. Bradman went on to make 205 not out and add another record to his tally. Had the appeal of Freeman and Ames been upheld, the psychological advantage might well have passed irreversibly to the bowlers of Kent and so of England, and the course of cricket history might have been changed.

By the end of the 1930 season Freeman had taken 846 wickets in three summers, surpassing anything that had been done before (Richardson's 1005 in four seasons was to be beaten the following year). He had also taken 2,080 wickets for Kent during his career. Colin Blythe's record still lay ahead of him, but still the cricket world marvelled that 'one small head could carry all he knew'.

His son, Percy, was being coached in the nets at Canterbury, but cricket was not to be for him. He became a traveller and settled later in the Midlands where 'Tich's' grand-daughter lives still. 'Tich' himself had become partner in a coaching school in Maidstone. His colleagues in the enterprise were Humphreys and Fenner. George Fenner was the father of the present Kent secretary and he was a shrewd and most efficient businessman. 'Tich' was neither of these things. He appeared irregularly at the coaching school, for his heart was always on the field rather than in the nets and he was too reticent ever to be a good coach. There was always a danger that, when he did appear, he would do more harm than good. George Fenner was less than pleased on one occasion when a wealthy customer approached 'Tich' and, pointing to a young boy he had with him, he said heartily, 'This is my son, Freeman, and I am going to give him into your care because I want you to turn him into a great bowler like yourself.'

'You can't coach bowlers,' said 'Tich', and walked away. He was only speaking what he believed to be true, but it was not very good business.

He was also involved in a sports outfitters in Maidstone which bore the name 'Hubble and Freeman'. His partner was the son of the old Kent wicket-keeper, but once more 'Tich' had no real interest in the business. He concerned himself less and less with what was happening and both parties were happy when he relinquished his share. It became a very lucrative concern.

'Tich' Freeman wanted only the beginning of the season when he could bustle back to the end of his five-pace run, eager to get at the batsman. In he would trot, the arm would come over as high as he could get it and the follow-through would be whip-like.

There was a time when 1931 promised great things for Kent. Under the leadership of Percy Chapman they played attractive and exciting cricket. They started brilliantly, struck a very bad patch

111

and then finished well to end third in the County Championship. For 'Tich' Freeman it was another marvellous year, and by the end of it four great records were his: he had passed Colin Blythe's record of 2231 wickets for Kent; he had established a new record aggregate of 1,122 wickets in four seasons; he had taken over 200 wickets for the fourth season in succession; and he had become the first bowler to take all ten wickets three times in first-class cricket, having accomplished all ten in an innings for the third season in succession.

In all he took 276 wickets in the season, the closest to him being Parker, naturally, with 219. There were four Kent players in the Gentlemen v. Players match at Lord's, but Freeman was not one of them. Peebles, Mitchell, Fender, F. R. Brown, Marriott, Stevens, whose bowling was now most uneconomical, and Robins were among the leg-break bowlers honoured during the season, not Freeman. He played for an England XI against the New Zealanders in the Folkestone Festival and took six wickets in the second innings, which no-one had accomplished in any of the Tests against them. When he played for Kent against the tourists at Canterbury he was injured after bowling only six overs in the first innings. He could not bat, but bounced back onto the field to take three wickets in the second innings and help Marriott to bowl Kent to victory.

The return of Marriott was obviously a great help to 'Tich', for his leg-break colleague had played no matches in 1930 due to illness. When Kent beat Notts at Dover in two days in mid-August these two took 19 of the wickets between them, and for once Marriott had the edge, getting ten to Freeman's nine. For Marriott, this partnership with 'Tich' was the delight of his cricketing life. When he joined the side 'Tich' always gave him a welcoming grin. The advantage of having them both in the side was that they were of contrasting styles, in both pace and height. Marriott was one of the quicker leg-break bowlers while 'Tich' bowled with a slow, high, tossed-up flight, though frequently he would bowl a quick 'fizzer' of flatter trajectory. They complemented each other and formed a deadly combination.

112

The third time that 'Tich' accomplished the feat of taking all ten wickets in an innings was at Old Trafford at the end of May; it is remarkable that Lancashire should twice have been on the receiving end of this performance at the hands of the same bowler within the space of three years. Hallows was bowled, Iddon stumped, Watson caught at slip and Hopwood bowled in quick succession as soon as 'Tich' came into the attack. Ernest Tyldesley and Eddie Paynter then added 80, but once he had caught and bowled Paynter, the rest of the Lancashire batting faded away before him and his final figures were 36.1−9−79−10.

At the end of 1931 season he stood, like Alexander, with no more worlds to conquer, yet there were still great years to come. Perhaps it is inappropriate to compare him to Alexander, who knew only too well the size of his empire, because 'Tich' never quite realised what he had achieved. Possibly it was the consistent rejection by Test selectors that caused him to diminish in his own mind the size of his accomplishment and there was neither the commercial involvement nor the media interest to inflate or to exploit what he had done. He just went on bowling because that was what he was happy doing.

Before the beginning of the 1932 season Lord Harris died and the following summer saw the death of Lieutenant-Colonel Lionel Troughton, so that two men who had been influential in 'Tich's' early years passed from the scene. He himself was now a veteran of 44, but in no way could this be offered as an argument for his non-selection for the first-ever Test match with India as Frank Woolley, a year his senior, was in the side. Woolley did not have a good season and Sir Home Gordon was moved to say, 'For the first time there was a retrogression in the batting of Frank Woolley... Compared with his old consistency, 1932 was for him a season of shreds and patches.'

The same could not be said of 'Tich' Freeman. Once more he was the leading wicket-taker in the country and, with 253 wickets, the only man to top the two hundred; Bill Bowes was next with 190. That Kent retained third place in the County Championship was almost entirely his doing. As the Kent seasonal review stated unequivocally, 'No other county was so weak in bowling as Kent, apart from Freeman.' The importance of 'Tich' to the Kent side can be seen from one statistic: he took 209 wickets in County Championship matches, which is exactly the same number that the 13 other players who bowled amassed between them.

There were some magic moments. In the week at Folkestone he took 30 wickets for 236 runs. The first match was against Lancashire. The week before, on 17 June, he had become the first bowler in the country to reach 100 wickets for the season, and now he destroyed the Red Rose county. At tea on the Saturday Lancashire were 193 for 4. They were all out for 219 shortly afterwards, Freeman 5 for 88. Kent batted consistently to reach 366. At tea on Monday Lancashire were 31 for 1. When play resumed at five o'clock, nine wickets went down for 91 runs. 'Tich' opened the bowling in the second innings and sent down 31 overs to take 8 for 56. Kent had won by an innings in two days.

The second match was against Warwickshire and he bowled unchanged from one end throughout the match. Kent made 174 and then 'Tich' took 8 for 31 to put Warwickshire out for 129. The two wickets that he did not get were opener G. D. Kemp-Welch who was run out for 9 and last man Mayer who was caught behind off Watt. Eventually, Warwickshire were set 215 to win, but only Wyatt could withstand Freeman on a wicket which gave some assistance to the bowler. He took 9 for 61 and once more Kent had won in two days. It was the second time in his career that he had taken 17 wickets in a match; only Walter Mead of Essex has also accomplished this feat twice. Les Ames tells of this match that so certain were the Warwickshire batsmen of their destruction that eight of them sat padded up waiting to go to the slaughter.

'Tich' did not play in the return game with Warwickshire at Edgbaston as he was in the Players' side at Lord's. It was not a match in which he particularly distinguished himself with the ball, but he did hit six fours in his innings of 31. His absence at Lord's gave a chance to D. V. P. Wright, a young leg-break bowler who had been showing good form in the 2nd XI.

For Kent it was good that at least one young bowler appeared to

114

be developing for there was general concern that there was little sign of the veterans being adequately replaced and that lean times were ahead. Ames, of course, was quite brilliant both with the bat and behind the stumps; he had 39 stumpings off 'Tich' and once more notched 100 dismissals. Chapman was his usual exuberant self, but his captaincy was prone to lapse in thought from time to time and was once severely criticised when, with a youngster bowling, he had Freeman, Woolley and Hardinge tearing about the outfield with combined ages of 135.

In his two games against the Indians Freeman bowled Kent and an England XI to victory, and was certainly more successful than Robins and Freddie Brown had been in the Test. Leg-break bowlers were still a vital part of Test cricket and in the 1931–32 series between Australia and South Africa it had been McMillan of South Africa, inevitably Grimmett, and a new young leg-spinner named Bill O'Reilly who had been the most successful bowlers.

Brown and Robins played against India; Brown and Mitchell of Derbyshire went to Australia with Jardine's team. Neither of them could compare with 'Tich', nor did their Test records come anywhere near his. Mitchell played in one Test in Australia when he was very sparingly used but took three wickets. O'Reilly had a splendid series, but this was the 'bodyline' era when for the first time cricketers began to believe that they could live by pace alone. In view of what 'Tich' Freeman was to do in 1933, this was even more ridiculous than it is today.

In 1928 'Tich' had bowled 11,857 balls. In 1933 he bowled 12,234, more in a single season than anyone before or since. His reward was 298 wickets, a total which had been bettered only by himself five years earlier. His wickets cost him only 15.26 runs apiece, and the next leading wicket-taker was Hedley Verity who had 108 fewer wickets. 'Tich' had reached 200 wickets by 14 August. This success in his forty-fifth year brought some angry comments from men of Kent to those who had disparaged the man and still undervalued his achievement. Sir Home Gordon once more championed him: 'His imperturbability, superb craft and skill speak for themselves. The fallacy of the assertion that he is ineffective against good batsmen surely needs no demonstration. If it were true, then three-fourths of the batsmen in county cricket are bad, which in these days when few counties have long "tails" is manifestly absurd.'

That Kent held on to third place was incredible after a dreadful start and was once more due mainly to the little man's efforts. The lack of support for him was severely felt, but still he bustled back to his mark, eager to deliver the leg-break pitched on leg stump and turning to hit off, or the googly for the unwary, or that lethal top-spinner which fizzed off the pitch and had all groping. Wickets came in profusion. There was 7 for 19 against Northants at Dover and 8 for 48 against Gloucestershire at Bristol (Hammond was top scorer with 55 before Ames stumped him off 'Tich'). There was a marvellous victory over the old enemy, Surrey, at Blackheath when he got 11 wickets, including Sandham in both innings and Hobbs in the first.

The best day, however, came in the last home Championship game of the season, against Yorkshire at Dover. Yorkshire were already champions for the third year running, but Kent hit a creditable 332. Yorkshire had lost only six wickets and were only two runs behind Kent when rain flooded the ground on Monday afternoon. On the resumption, Yorkshire gained the three runs needed for first-innings lead at which point Brian Sellers declared to give Macaulay, Verity and Leyland a chance to exploit the drying wicket. Verity took nine wickets and Kent were bowled out for 133, so leaving the champions needing that score to win. Freeman and Marriott opened the bowling. Holmes and Sutcliffe began quite well, but then wickets began to tumble. 'Tich' had 6 for 51 and Marriott 3 for 36, and Kent won by 44 runs.

It was during this season that 'Tich' first bowled in harness with Doug Wright, and there were to be occasions in the future when Kent were to field three leg-break bowlers in the same side. The third was Charles Marriott, a good bowler, a terrible bat and an awful fielder. His greatest cricketing pleasure was bowling with 'Tich', to whom he regularly paid tribute. In 1933, he took 54 wickets at 18.44 each. He was, of course, only available in the school holidays.

The England selectors had adopted a mixed policy towards the sides that they chose to meet the West Indies that season, hardened campaigners filling most spots but with a sprinkling of newcomers. R. W. V. Robins, who had been unavailable to tour Australia the previous winter, was the leg-break bowler chosen for the first two Tests; C. S. Marriott was chosen for the third Test. He had a remarkable game with match figures of 11 for 96 and was chosen to tour India the following winter, but he never played in another Test match. What one finds so bewildering about the selection is that Marriott was 38 years old when he was chosen. It was not a question of experimenting with a youngster. His talent was well-known and he was certainly no better in 1933 than he had been four years earlier. It was also well-known that he was certainly not as good a bowler as his Kent colleague. His selection takes its place in the enigmatic pattern. Les Ames and Howard Levett are still stunned by it; no-one will ever know what 'Tich' felt.

What the Kent Committee thought about 'Tich' was soon made apparent as they granted him a second benefit in 1934. It was a gesture not only to the man who had carried the Kent bowling on his shoulders for several years but also to one who had raised much money for Kent charities by arranging matches in which he, of course, was always a participant. Once more Kent followers had an opportunity to show their appreciation of the untiring enthusiasm of the little man. With never a hair out of place, albeit there were fewer of them, and a quiet smile for everyone, he had become a folk philosopher, not through pronouncement but through action. His second benefit was to bring him £1586 2s 2d which was more than either Ashdown a year later or Les Ames in 1937 was to receive.

Once more in 1934 he was the only bowler to top 200 wickets. He had 205 and big Jim Smith of Middlesex was next with 172, but Alf's wickets were bought at a greater cost than they had been for many years. So limited was the Kent bowling, Watt proving very expensive, that 'Tich' opened the bowling often, not as a tactic but as a necessity. His smile was still there, but there was also a nagging foot injury towards the end of the season and Don Bradman hit him for 30 in an over at Folkestone.

There were still some great days. At the first county cricket match at Brentwood in modern times, in which 1414 runs were scored and only 24 wickets fell, 'Tich' had 11 of them for 176. Then there was the third hat-trick of his career, against Surrey at Blackheath. This was a memorable match, 'Tich' finishing with 8 for 136 (only Sandham and Gregory avoided him) and Kent, inspired by Woolley, scoring 416 to win. Woolley was also to the fore in the game with Northants at Dover. This was one of those occasions when Freeman and Marriott worked as a pair but all the honours went to Freeman. Marriott sent down three more overs than his friend, but Freeman took 14 for 206 while Marriott had 3 for 132. Woolley hit a hundred in 63 minutes to give Kent victory.

Woolley found himself recalled to the England side for the final Test, but it was not a happy return. He made four and nought and had to keep wicket when Ames was injured. By this time, Woolley's slip-fielding to the quicker bowlers was not what it had been in his younger days, but he still held the catches off 'Tich's' bowling and, indeed, in 1935 he held 22 catches off the leg-spinner. He stood much closer for 'Tich's' bowling than was customary, but he had stood there for years and for him, as for Ames, fielding to 'Tich' had by now become second nature.

In the aftermath of bodyline England were in something of a mess and although Verity bowled them to victory at Lord's, they lost the series to Australia by two Tests to one. The selectors had moved into the pace mania, quick or medium, and although Verity was their most successful bowler, the only other spinner to play was the Derbyshire googly bowler, Mitchell, who played in the first and fourth Tests and took one wicket, that of Oldfield, at a cost of 225 runs. The Australian attack meanwhile consisted almost entirely of the leg-spin of Grimmett and O'Reilly who captured 25 and 28 wickets respectively, next highest being Wall with six wickets. Both of the leg-spinners took over 100 wickets on the tour as did the unorthodox left-arm spinner, Fleetwood-Smith. Like the rest of the cricket world, 'Tich' must sometimes have

118

wondered what crime he had long since committed that excluded
him from ever getting an opportunity to play against Australia in
England.

11
The Last Years, 1935–65

During the winter of 1934–35, the Advisory County Cricket Committee decided by a substantial majority to give a trial to a new leg-before-wicket law. The new law was: 'The striker is out lbw if with any part of his person (except his hand), which is between wicket and wicket, he intercepts a ball which in the opinion of the umpire at the bowler's wicket, shall have been pitched in a straight line from the bowler's wicket to the striker's wicket or shall have been pitched on the off-side of the striker's wicket and would have hit it.'

The thinking behind the new law was to encourage off-side play. Few realised that it was the second nail in the coffin of the leg-break bowler. Within a year, R. E. S. Wyatt, then captain of England, was to criticise the law as encouraging off-break and in-swing bowling and thereby discouraging off-side play. Years later, 'Gubby' Allen was to look back and describe the new law as the most disastrous piece of cricket legislation in his lifetime, producing as it did a race of front-footed batsmen and bringing about a decline in off-side play and the demise of the leg-spinner. No cricketers seemed to welcome it, so why it was ever introduced is hard to imagine, but then the rules are frequently tampered with for no good reason.

120

'Tich' himself certainly did not see the danger, but neither did he welcome the new law, being quoted in the *Morning Post* as saying, 'No change is needed; but if a change is made, some of us might get an absurd number of wickets each year.' In fact, the percentage of wickets obtained by lbw decisions in 1935 was no greater than it had been in some earlier seasons. For the eighth successive season he was the leading wicket-taker in the country, taking 212 wickets in all matches at a cheaper cost than in the previous year. In his forty-seventh year the burden he carried was more immense than ever, and there were occasions when it seemed agonising to some of those watching that he should bear such a load without rest. At Hastings, for example, he was kept on almost throughout the innings while 419 runs were scored, and still he smiled and was unruffled. Certainly if he was tired or in pain, he never showed it. An injury to Marriott did not help to lessen Freeman's burden.

One thing that was now apparent was that 'Tich' bowled the googly less and less. There had always seemed a reluctance, or lack of confidence, to use it against the very best batsmen, the top-spinner being preferred. It should be remembered, though, that Bradman's vulnerability, for example, was thought to be the leg-break, not the googly; it was with the leg break that 'Tich' had become the first Englishman to dismiss him, and it was with the leg-break that Peebles got him. The criticism of Peebles had been that if he had been able to bowl the leg-break more amid his plethora of googlies, he would have given the Don even more trouble. Les Ames recalls hitting a century against 'Tich' in a festival match and never once receiving a googly but perhaps, as Les admits, it was because 'Tich' knew he could read his every delivery.

The faith in leg-break bowlers was reasserted in the Tests where Robins, Sims and Mitchell all played, though with limited success. Eric Hollies had been with Wyatt's team in the West Indies during the preceding winter.

In spite of the new lbw law, leg-break bowlers had the lion's share of wickets, for apart from 'Tich's' 216, there were among

121

others Robins (80), Hollies (130), Mitchell (171), Peebles (50), Sims (131), Marriott (34), Owen-Smith (38), Cameron (60), Peter Smith (66), Brown (61) and Fender (66).

The contrast with the 1981 season is pronounced, yet the change was neither dramatic nor sudden. The leg-break bowler was to hold his place in cricket for several years after the introduction of the new lbw law. Robins, a sparkling captain of Middlesex, was to lead England in 1937 and Peebles succeeded him as captain of the county (Arthur Mailey had always asserted that only leg-break bowlers were really fit to skipper a side). The England party to Australia in 1936–37 included two leg-break bowlers, Robins and Sims, and, not surprisingly, O'Reilly was the leading wicket-taker for Australia in the series.

In 1938, Doug Wright became a Test player and for his entire Test career he remained the bowler most likely to capture a wicket at any time, in any conditions. Two leg-break bowlers were in the party to tour South Africa in the winter of 1938, Wright being joined by Wilkinson of Lancashire. Both bowlers were in the England side for the third Test of the series, which England won, the only one of the five to have a positive result. Wright was also in the England side for the series against the West Indies which was played in the last season before the outbreak of the second world war. One interesting fact about that series is that leg-break bowler C. B. Clarke proved effective for West Indies and in the third Test, Len Hutton dismissed Jeffrey Stollmeyer. This was one of three Test wickets that Len Hutton took in his career, but it should be remembered that in all first-class cricket he took 173 wickets and that in 1939, with his leg-breaks, he took 44 wickets at 18.68 runs each. It is true to say that this form of attack was never really fashionable with Yorkshire, but Hutton was used to effect when it suited.

The years immediately after the second world war showed little change from what had gone before. When Hammond's team went to Australia in 1946–47 there were two leg-break bowlers, Wright and Peter Smith, in the 17 and the Kent man was England's leading bowler in the Tests. Australia confronted

122

England with McCool and Dooland. McCool in particular was a great success. It was the general feeling that the English batsmen were most vulnerable against leg-spin bowling. Both Dooland and McCool were later to play in English county cricket.

When the Australians arrived in 1948 for their first post-war tour of England they were confronted by a rule which allowed them a new ball in Test matches every 55 overs. Lindwall, Miller and Bill Johnston were able to bowl almost throughout the innings, Toshack and Ian Johnson sending down a few perfunctory overs of containment. McCool and his fellow leg-spinner, Ring, had become superfluous. Wright played in only one Test and England lost a glorious opportunity of beating Australia at Leeds when they caught the visitors on a turning wicket and had only the inexperienced off-breaks of Jim Laker at their disposal. The final irony came in the fifth Test at The Oval. In his last innings in Test cricket Don Bradman was bowled second ball by a googly from leg-spinner Hollies for nought.

In South Africa, Wright and particularly Roly Jenkins had great success, but the flame of the leg-break bowler was already burning lower. Peebles and Wilkinson had returned very briefly after the war and by the early 'fifties Sims and Peter Smith had disappeared from first-class cricket. Robins, Brown, who later indulged in seam, Hollies, Jenkins, Wright and, after an all too brief career, Leadbeater all retired from the game before the end of the 'fifties. When he left the game Douglas Wright had established a record of seven hat-tricks in first-class cricket.

Greenough struggled on for Lancashire until 1966, and there was Bob Barber, an exciting batsman, who took over 40 wickets in his 28 Tests with his leg-breaks, but the art was dying, in England at least. There was still an adherence to the faith overseas. Ramadhin bowled both off-breaks and leg-breaks, and Richie Benaud emerged as one of the great Australian spinners in the Mailey, Grimmett and O'Reilly line, a tradition which Jim Higgs is striving to maintain. Mushtaq and Intikhab in Pakistan and Gupte and Chandrasekhar in India flourished, but in England the flame was now all but extinguished.

Robin Hobbs was an anachronism and that he played in seven Test matches was remarkable, but even he found it difficult to overcome prejudices. In 1970 he was one of only three bowlers to take 100 wickets in the season, a season in which Latchman for Middlesex and Tidy for Warwickshire also bowled leg-breaks to advantage. When the team to tour Australia was announced, however, it was discovered that the place which most had believed would go to Hobbs had gone to Don Wilson of Yorkshire, left-arm, who with just over 50 wickets, taken at a much dearer cost than those that Hobbs had obtained, was considered a 'safer' bet.

A parsimony, which many felt had first shown itself in 'Tich' Freeman's last year as Test player, was now at high tide. It was fostered by the increasing financial rewards which were being offered to successful cricket teams and cricketers and which made it as profitable to prevent batsmen from scoring runs as to take their wickets. The limited-over game, constructed for commerce and instant thrills, has produced negative bowling, defensive field placings and some unaesthetic batting. When a spinner operates in the limited-over game he invariably does little more than roll his fingers over the top of the ball and bowl flat at the leg stump. Spinning fingers rarely become raw, sore or blistered these days, for they are rarely used. Whatever the intentions in the three-day game, it becomes more and more difficult to play Hyde one day and Jekyll the next.

By the nature of his art, the leg-break bowler is unable to make compromises. He is an attacker who dangles bait and lures to destruction by subtlety. When he is used defensively, as Intikhab has been in recent times, he loses the ability to spin the ball.

Not only the social factors of cricket but the physical and legislative ones have acted against the leg-spinner. The use of artificial fertilisers, the increased lushness of outfields keeping the ball 'new' for longer, the loss of natural wickets for a variety of reasons, all have told against the leg-spinner so that the desire to master this difficult art is dried up by the realisation that, even if the skill is attained, there may be little or no opportunity to use it. At school level, the leg-spinner is still the most prolific wicket-taker (Colin Cowdrey was a lethal leg-break bowler at Tonbridge), but as he grows older he concentrates on his batting or turns to medium pace. The incentive to continue, in all but some club cricket, is gone.

The hope, of course, is that in all declines there is the spark of a renaissance. If a leg-break bowler learns his art in the right way and by hard practice, as 'Tich' did, there is no reason whatever why he should be any less accurate or any more of a gamble than any other type of bowler.

It was 75 years ago that Albert Knight of Leicestershire and England wrote, 'Leg-break spin from right to left is not so easy of accomplishment, or rather to maintain the indispensable length at which alone it is effective is a very difficult art. The ball when delivered is underneath the hand, slipping out as it were when fingers and wrist have turned the ball over. Hence pace, the strength needed for propulsion, is rarely found conjoined with the leg-break. Nearly all of us can bowl a ball with a big leg-break in the nets, but ''fear seizeth upon them and trouble'' when the nets are removed and a match game substituted. The leg-break ball when bowled is one presenting greater difficulty than the off-break. One can always get more leg-break spin, even on the most perfect of wickets, than off-break. The batsman too is not as a rule sufficiently clever with his feet as to permit him to get so clear and distinct a view of the leg ball as is essential for a correct judgment of its length.

'Nothing in fact is more difficult to play correctly than a perfect leg-break.'

A generation of batsmen is coming to the crease which has no experience in coping with leg-break bowling, and is it fanciful to hope that a young bowler may arise who will confound them as 'Tich' Freeman confounded all batsmen in England from 1928 until 1935?

The beginning of the 1936 season suggested that all was as it had been for the past eight seasons. The first two months of the season brought 'Tich' 79 wickets and Kent won their first four matches

125

in fine style. 'Tich' had 3 for 23 and 5 for 109 against Gloucestershire at Gravesend and followed this by destroying Derbyshire, the eventual champions, on the same ground. Kent won in two days and he had match figures of 9 for 52. Then there was 11 for 145 at Edgbaston and all seemed right with the world.

In fact it was the final flourish. In the last two months of the season 'Tich' took only 29 wickets to finish with only 110 wickets at 25.41 each, 108 of them being taken for Kent. The truth was all too apparent. 'This wonderful bowler, famed for never-flagging perseverance as much as for skill in spinning and flighting his slows, at last, when 47 years of age, suffered from the strain of putting his right arm to such exacting exertion. His muscles could not bear the work.'

Howard Levett remembers that last season well and remembers above all that 'Tich's' googly had almost disappeared. 'I think it hurt him,' he says, 'but he never said. Mind you, Alf would never have said if anything hurt him.' It is easy to tear a muscle in shoulder or elbow when bowling the googly and Alf was obviously feeling the strain of years of endeavour. 'We played Middlesex at Maidstone,' Howard Levett goes on, 'and it was the first time we had come up against Denis Compton. He was only a youngster and he got 80-odd in the first innings and looked to be on his way to a hundred in the second. I kept saying to Alf, ''Give him the 'google'. He's only a youngster.'' But he never did. That's when I realised it hurt him.'

Denis recalls the match, too. 'I had heard so much about the man that I was looking for the googly from the moment I went in. It never came. In the end he got me caught behind by ''Hopper'' Levett off a straightforward leg-break.'

All endings are sad. Even in the greatest of comedies from *Twelfth Night* to *City Lights* the final scenes have an unbearable poignancy. 'Tich's' end in first-class cricket was no exception. A cricket season without him wheeling away seemed unthinkable. The Kent Committee suggested that he should be engaged on a match-to-match basis; he would be played in certain games and have periods of rest in between. That was not something that Alf understood, his appetite for bowling was still so great, and he declined. The Kent Committee was left with no alternative and in the November it was announced that he was not to be re-engaged. His first-class career was at an end.

His last game for Kent was in the Folkestone Festival, against MCC. In the second innings he took his last wicket for them, Mr R. de W. K. Winlaw, stumped by Howard Levett for 39.

He had two more games to play, both at Folkestone, for an England XI against India and, lastly, for the Players against the Gentlemen. He bowled Mr M. Tindall for 39 in the second innings and then he was gone from first-class cricket, the man who mastered the art of leg-break and googly bowling as no one else has ever done. His record speaks for itself, it is unapproachable, and no silly arguments can detract from it. He allied perfect length, varied flight, subtlety of delivery and stamina to an ability to impart the right amount of spin needed for his purpose. This is a quality that 'Father' Marriott says that he had to learn the hard way. Shortly after he began his career with Kent, he and 'Tich' caught Middlesex on a sticky wicket at Blackheath. Woolley picked up five catches at slip and in his excitement Marriott began to try to spin the ball more and more. The result was that he lost his length and the ball was savaged to the boundary. Woolley glared at him and 'Tich' frowned. He came to his senses and he and 'Tich' bowled Middlesex out. 'Tich' did not lose control in circumstances like this.

At the end of the season Chapman resigned from the Kent captaincy. An era which gave joy to many was over.

Wisden carried a special resumé of Freeman's career in the 1937 annual, pointing out that his 3,775 wickets in first-class cricket stood second only to Rhodes' 4,184, but that whereas Rhodes had had 29 seasons to reach his total, 'Tich' had had only 19.

There was genuine regret at his departure. Cricket was left with a void. E. W. Swanton, the most perceptive and precise of writers, noted succinctly the sight that had graced the counties for 19 seasons: 'There was something grotesque in the way the little gnome of a man came rocking up to the stumps, and flicked one ball after another, all so nearly the same, and yet so vitally different, until the victim would either commit some act of indiscretion or, more probably, fall to his own timidity.'

Following his retirement from the first-class game, Alf Freeman spent a couple of years with Walsall in the Birmingham and District League and then retired to a house in Maidstone which he called, appropriately, 'Dunbolyn'. The name of Freeman lingered a little while longer in Kent scorebooks. Alf's nephew, recorded rather austerely as D. P. Freeman, played in the game against Somerset at Bath in June 1937. Batting at no. 8, he scored 4 and 6. He was not re-engaged after the 1938 season.

Then came the period immediately after the second world war, a boom time for cricket. Crowds flocked to see the ageing giants of the past, like Wally Hammond who could still score 1,783 runs in a season and average 84.90, and the vigorous new generation of heroes like Edrich and Compton. There was celebration in the air and 1946 was the centenary of the Surrey County Cricket Club. Part of the festivities took the form of a special match, Surrey v. Old England.

It was a glorious day, 23 May, and 15,000 people, including King George VI, turned out to see the match. Hobbs and Strudwick umpired, and the Old England side was Sutcliffe, Sandham, Woolley, Hendren, Jardine, Fender, D. J. Knight, Tate, E. R. T. Holmes, Allom, Brooks (the former Surrey keeper and only non-Test player in the side) and 'Tich' Freeman. Including Hobbs and Strudwick, there were 370 Test caps on display for Old England.

The match was a great success and warmed many hearts. The Old England players were given a great reception and Percy Fender, who captained the side, wrote a letter to *The Times* in which he expressed the gratitude of all concerned. He felt that the reception the old players had received was a message to all young cricketers, 'a message telling them that where cricket is concerned, public memory, in spite of the old adage, is not short'.

128

It certainly was not short as far as 'Tich' was concerned. He took Laurie Fishlock's wicket, bowled 15 overs and conceded 58 runs. Woolley, Hendren and Jardine scored runs and the match was excitingly, and rightly, drawn.

Three years later, at a Special General Meeting of the MCC at Lord's on 14 July 1949, it was decided unanimously to offer Honorary Cricket Membership of the club to 26 former professionals who, in the opinion of the MCC, had given great service to the game. It was a distinguished list that was announced. Hirst and Rhodes were there, and S. F. Barnes, and Woolley and Hobbs and Larwood, and so was Alfred Percy Freeman. The game had paid him its final honour.

He turned out from time to time in charity games. Maurice Fenner, the present Kent secretary, remembers playing with him in the early 'fifties. 'Tich', then past 60, captained the side and dropped the first ball he bowled straight on a length.

Often he would be driven to matches when Kent were at home and would sit in the car and watch, his head just visible above the dashboard. Doug Wright would have a chat with him when possible, but he would rarely leave the car. He had become asthmatic (too many Passing Clouds?) and he simply wanted to watch in peace the game he loved beyond all else in life. He never joined the lads in the pavilion for a drink after the match, for Ethel was waiting to take him home at the close of play.

'Tich' Freeman died on 28 January 1965, within three months of his seventy-seventh birthday. Kent players, past and present, joined to honour him at his funeral. The procession was late in arriving at the chapel. 'Perhaps Ethel wouldn't let him come,' said one of his contemporaries. All smiled. It was neither a vindictive nor an irreligious quip, but simply an observation of affection for two people who had been part of Kent cricket, and of the lives of all those present.

Later the same year, on the Monday of Canterbury week, 2 August, a wall plaque was unveiled at Canterbury which honoured the man and commemorated his achievements. It was the third year running that a plaque had been unveiled at Canterbury and

'Tich' took his place alongside his friends, Les Ames and Frank Woolley. It was a dreadful day. Only one hour's play was possible in Kent's match with Hampshire and the heavens seemed to be lamenting the passing of the great, little man. Having been introduced by the President of the Kent Club, J. A. Deed, Lord Cornwallis, one of 'Tich's' first captains, performed the ceremony. There was a good gathering, including 'Tich's' son, Percy, and Lord Cornwallis told them that it was 'Tich's' great accuracy and stamina that enabled him to hold so many cricketing records; it was doubtful if many of them would ever be broken. He added that he thought if 'Tich' had been playing today, he would have taken 400 wickets in a season because the majority of present day batsmen failed to use their feet and they would have been easy prey for 'Tich'.

Most of his contemporaries agree with this assessment. There was only one man who ever really defeated 'Tich' with consistency and that was Duleepsinhji. The story goes that the Maidstone wicket had been over-watered at one end for the match against Sussex in 1929 and the visitors were shot out for 69, 'Tich' taking 7 for 16. The Kent authorities were most apologetic, but Duleepsinhji vowed revenge on his journey back to Sussex, and he exacted it.

'Tich's' monument is not just the plaque at Canterbury, nor the imposing list of records. He is remembered in the hearts of all those who knew him, and by many who never even saw him. Colin Page, now director of coaching for Kent, who knew him only towards the end, says simply, 'Lovely little man.' And there are those whose fathers and grandfathers watched Kent cricket and who were brought up with Freeman's name and deeds as an integral part of their childhood. 'He bowled all day. There was never anybody like him. Never will be again.'

When the proposal for this study of the great bowler was mooted to the sales department of one publisher, it was dismissed, somewhat contemptuously, as 'wickets in the sky'. It is a lovely thought, and one thing is certain: if there is cricket in heaven, a little man of five feet, two inches will be hurrying back to his mark, hitching up his trousers with his forearms, and bowling off five paces from 11.30 in the morning until 6.30 in the evening.

And Ethel will be there to collect him at the close.

David Lemmon
Leigh-on Sea
1981

Appendix

The Career Record of A. P. Freeman

The author is indebted to Kent County Cricket Club and to the work of John F. Griffiths for their groundwork in compiling these statistics.

BATTING

	Matches	Inns	N.O.	Runs	H.S.	Ave.
For Kent	506	630	170	4257	66*	9.29
Other in England ...	44	37	7	296	32*	9.86
Overseas	44	49	17	360	57	11.25
Total	594	716	194	4913	66*	9.40

66* v. Lancs, Manchester, 1925
57 MCC v. South Australia, Adelaide, 1922–23
Twice made 'spectacles'

BOWLING

	Wickets	Runs	Ave.	10 wkts match	5 wkts inns
For Kent	3340	58944	17.64	123	348
Other in England ...	242	5669	23.42	8	24
Overseas	194	4964	25.58	4	14
Total	3776	69577	18.42	135	386

DISMISSALS – 1456 ct, 104 ct & b, 1053 b. 651 lbw, 484 st, 28 hw
48.6% of all wickets taken were without assistance
(ct & b, b, lbw, hw).
Freeman delivered 154,743 balls in his career.

FIELDING

Kent – 203 catches; Other in England 10; Overseas 24 ct, 1 st.
Total 237 ct, 1 st.

KENT

Year	Balls	R.	W.	Ave	10 w/m	5 w/i	ct	c&b	b	lbw	st	hw
1914	1300	799	29	27.55	–	2	8	2	9	5	5	–
1919	2165	1209	60	20.15	2	4	22	2	21	8	6	1
1920	3909	1722	102	16.88	–	4	35	1	36	16	14	–
1921	5858	2939	163	18.03	6	14	55	5	58	24	16	5
1922	6607	2839	194	14.63	8	16	77	3	66	27	20	1
1923	5940	2642	157	16.82	1	9	61	1	56	29	9	1
1924	5942	2425	159	15.25	2	12	51	7	52	28	19	2
1925	6433	2544	146	17.42	4	14	64	4	49	19	9	1
1926	7876	3603	177	20.35	5	18	68	9	50	28	20	2
1927	6978	3153	173	18.22	5	18	79	4	44	27	18	1
1928	9281	4325	246	17.58	13	30	102	8	57	43	36	–
1929	7818	3729	214	17.42	10	22	91	8	53	25	37	–
1930	10505	4153	260	15.97	15	34	97	6	66	50	39	2
1931	8930	3932	257	15.29	13	33	96	9	70	49	31	2
1932	8386	3442	226	15.23	12	26	65	4	61	53	41	2
1933	10978	3862	262	14.74	15	35	99	5	53	67	35	3
1934	10007	4470	195	22.92	7	22	69	3	57	40	26	–
1935	9019	4562	212	21.51	9	25	85	6	42	42	36	1
1936	5148	2594	108	24.01	1	10	45	2	37	10	13	1
	133080	58944	3340	17.64	128	348	1269	89	937	590	430	25
				as %			38	2.6	28	17.6	13	0.8

		KENT Ct	St	Total	ALL Ct	St	Total
Woolley	...	203	–	203	219	–	219
Ashdown	...	141	–	141	141	–	141
Hardinge	...	70	–	70	71	–	71
Chapman	...	62	–	62	68	–	68
Todd	...	59	–	59	59	–	59
Valentine	...	56	–	56	57	–	57
Ames	...	94	237	331	100	259	359
Hubble	...	52	107	159	52	107	159
Levett	...	24	65	89	24	68	92

Les Ames kept wicket in 247 games for Kent in all, dismissing 697 batsmen (ct 374, st 323). Howard Levett played 121 games for Kent and he dismissed 354 batsmen (ct 193, st 161).

OTHER

	Balls	R.	W.	10/5	ct	c&b	b	lbw	st	hw
1914	–									
1919	–									
1920	126	68	–	–						
1921	246	147	3	–	2	–	–	–	1	–
1922	–									
1923	–									
1924	192	93	8	–/1	4	–	1	3	–	–
1925	–									
1926	235	137	3	–	1	–	2	–	–	–
1927	409	177	8	–	6	–	1	1	–	–
1928	2543	1164	58	2/6	28	–	12	12	6	–
1929	2184	1150	53	3/7	27	2	14	4	6	–
1930	922	479	15	–	2	–	11	2	–	–
1931	778	375	19	–/2	6	1	9	2	1	–
1932	997	707	27	1/2	10	–	5	3	9	–
1933	1259	687	36	2/5	14	–	6	8	7	1
1934	461	283	10	–/1	4	–	2	2	2	–
1935	–									
1936	258	202	2	–	–	–	1	1	–	–
	10610	5669	242	8/24	104	3	64	38	32	1

OVERSEAS

	Balls	R.	W.	10/5	ct	c&b	b	lbw	st	hw
Australia & N.Z.										
1922–23	3698	1654	69	2/5	29	6	21	5	7	1
Australia										
1924–25	2600	1209	40	–/2	16	4	12	6	2	–
South Africa										
1927–28	2318	965	50	2/4	26	2	10	8	3	1
Australia										
1928–29	2437	1136	35	–/3	12	–	9	4	10	–
	11053	4964	194	4/14	83	12	52	23	22	2

FOR KENT

TEAMS	TOTAL				HOME				AWAY			
	W.	R.	Ave.	10m/5i	W.	R.	Ave.	10m/5i	W.	R.	Ave.	10m/5i
Derbyshire	178	3025	16.99	7/22	92	1344	14.60	4/12	86	1681	19.54	3/10
Essex	269	4427	16.45	13/32	149	2192	14.71	8/18	120	2235	18.62	5/14
Glamorgan	71	935	13.16	5/10	35	462	13.20	2/5	36	473	13.13	3/5
Gloucestershire ...	241	3497	14.51	14/33	101	1534	15.18	5/11	140	1963	14.02	9/19
Hampshire	226	4878	21.58	6/22	120	2400	20.00	2/11	106	2478	23.37	4/11
Lancashire	168	4122	24.53	6/12	111	2490	22.43	5/10	57	1632	28.63	1/2
Leicestershire ...	231	2679	11.59	12/23	127	1393	10.96	6/12	104	1286	12.36	6/11
Middlesex	220	4265	19.38	7/21	119	2164	18.18	4/11	101	2099	20.78	3/10
Northamptonshire ...	253	2965	11.71	12/30	119	1357	11.40	4/11	134	1608	12.00	8/19
Nottinghamshire ...	153	3302	21.58	3/13	91	1626	17.86	3/8	62	1676	27.03	–/5
Somerset	208	2936	14.11	7/22	97	1254	12.92	2/10	111	1682	15.15	5/12
Surrey	142	3701	26.06	3/12	82	2113	25.76	3/9	60	1588	26.46	–/3
Sussex	244	4498	18.43	9/15	118	2079	17.61	4/12	126	2419	19.19	5/13
Warwickshire ...	212	3412	16.09	7/22	122	1849	15.15	4/13	90	1563	17.36	3/9
Worcestershire ...	188	2895	15.39	7/18	95	1374	14.46	4/10	93	1521	16.35	3/8
Yorkshire	147	3006	20.44	5/14	92	1931	20.98	3/9	55	1075	19.54	2/5
MCC	59	1604	27.92	2/5	53	1480	27.92	2/5	6	124	20.66	–/1
Cambridge Univ. ...	8	82	10.25	–/1	–	–	–	–	8	82	10.25	–/1
Oxford Univ. ...	45	907	20.15	1/5	–	–	–	–	45	907	20.15	1/5
Australia	15	508	33.86	–/2	15	508	33.86	–/2	–	–	–	–
India	12	218	18.16	–/1	12	218	18.16	–/1	–	–	–	–
New Zealand ...	11	271	18.06	–/1	11	271	18.06	–/1	–	–	–	–
South Africa ...	10	303	30.30	–/1	10	303	30.30	–/1	–	–	–	–
West Indies	24	367	15.29	2/3	24	367	15.29	2/3	–	–	–	–
Aust. Imp. Forces...	5	141	28.20	–	5	141	28.20	–	–	–	–	–
Totals	3340	58944	17.64	128/348	1800	30850	17.13	65/185	1540	28094	18.24	63/163

BOWLING DETAILS—KENT GROUNDS

KENT MATCHES

		Wkts	Runs	Ave.
Blackheath	......	97	2306	23.77
Canterbury	......	350	6297	17.99
Chatham	......	21	352	16.76
Dover	......	218	4286	19.66
Folkestone	......	195	3562	18.26
Gravesend	......	221	3227	14.60
Maidstone	......	210	3398	16.18
Tonbridge	......	278	4263	15.33
Tunbridge Wells	...	210	3159	15.04
Totals	......	1800	30850	17.13

ALL MATCHES

		Wkts	Runs	Ave.
Folkestone	......	329	6643	20.19

BEST ANALYSES

INNINGS

5 wkts (153 times) 12 runs v. Northants, Gravesend, 1928
                    14 runs v. Leics, Tunbridge Wells, 1920
6 wkts (129 times) 18 runs v. Glos, Cheltenham, 1922
7 wkts (61 times)   11 runs v. Leics, Leicester, 1929
                    16 runs v. Sussex, Maidstone, 1929
                    19 runs v. Northants, Dover, 1933
                    20 runs v. Glos, Cheltenham, 1924
8 wkts (35 times)   22 runs v. Northants, Northampton, 1921
                    22 runs   S. of Eng. v. MCC, Folkestone, 1933
          (10 times Freeman took 8 wkts for 48 runs or less)
9 wkts (5 times)   11 runs v. Sussex, Hove, 1922
                    50 runs v. Derby, Ilkeston, 1930
                    61 runs v. Warwicks, Folkestone, 1932
                    87 runs v. Sussex, Hastings, 1920 (inn. dec.)
                   104 runs v. W. Indies, Canterbury, 1928
10 wkts (3 times)   53 runs v. Essex, Southend, 1930
                    79 runs v. Lancs, Manchester, 1931
                   131 runs v. Lancs, Manchester, 1929

MATCHES

10 wkts (34 times)	76 runs	(3-41, 7-35) v. Glos, Tonbridge, 1922
11 wkts (39 times)	42 runs	(4-31, 7-11) v. Leics, Leicester, 1929
	59 runs	(4-40, 7-19) v. Northants, Dover, 1933
	60 runs	(5-18, 6-42) v. Glos, Folkestone, 1933
12 wkts (27 times)	71 runs	(6-35, 6-36) v. Sussex, Tunbridge Wells, 1922
	72 runs	(6-18, 6-54) v. Glos, Cheltenham, 1922
13 wkts (21 times)	67 runs	(8-22, 5-45) v. Northants, Northampton, 1921
	83 runs	(7-60, 6-23) v. Leics, Leicester, 1932
	84 runs	(7-42, 6-42) v. Glam, Canterbury, 1932
14 wkts (10 times)	115 runs	(7-41, 7-74) v. Essex, Gravesend, 1935
15 wkts (5 times)	94 runs	(7-59, 8-35) v. Somerset, Canterbury, 1931
	122 runs	(8-64, 7-58) v. Middx, Lord's, 1933
	142 runs	(8-109, 7-33) v. Essex, Gravesend, 1931
	144 runs	(8-52, 7-92) v. Leics, Maidstone, 1931
	224 runs	8-64, 7-160) v. Leics, Tonbridge, 1928
16 wkts (twice)	82 runs	(8-44, 8-38) v. Northants, Tunbridge Wells, 1932
	94 runs	(10-53, 6-41) v. Essex, Southend, 1930
17 wkts (twice)	67 runs	(9-11, 8-56) v. Sussex, Hove, 1922
	92 runs	(8-31, 9-61) v. Warwicks, Folkestone, 1932

HAT-TRICKS
v. Middlesex, Canterbury, 1920
MCC v. South Australia, Adelaide, 1922-23
v. Surrey, Blackheath, 1934

EXPENSIVE ANALYSES
0 wkts 169 runs England v. South Africa, Oval, 1929
1 wkt 175 runs v. Notts, Canterbury, 1935

OVER 200 RUNS IN INNINGS
4 wkts 245 runs MCC v. Victoria, Melbourne, 1928–29
6 wkts 208 runs England XI v. W. Indies, Folkestone, 1933

MOST RUNS IN MATCH
8 wkts 331 runs v. MCC, Folkestone, 1934
8 wkts 268 runs MCC v. South Australia, Adelaide, 1922–23

OUTSTANDING SPELLS OF WICKET-TAKING

3 innings	25 wkts 148 runs (8-38, 8-31, 9-61)	1932
2 matches	30 wkts 236 runs (above plus 5-88)	1932
	29 wkts 139 runs (12-72, 17-67)	1922
3 matches	41 wkts 451 runs (14-198, 13-110, 14-143)	1930
6 innings	46 wkts 429 runs	
	(8-56, 3 innings, 5-143, 8-44, 8-38)	1932
7 innings	51 wkts 517 runs (6 innings, plus 5-88)	1932
4 matches	53 wkts 582 runs (3 matches, plus 12-131)	1930
5 matches	64 wkts 664 runs (above plus 11-82)	1930
7 matches	83 wkts 947 runs (above plus 8-123, 11-160	1930
9 matches	104 wkts 1287 runs (5 matches plus 12-130,	
	10-186, 12-210, 6-97)	1930

104 wkts from 21 May to 20 June 1930. This is, perhaps, the only time 100 wkts have been taken during a one-month period. 91 wkts in June, 1930; 36 wkts in September 1933; 10 or more wkts in 7 consecutive County Championship matches in 1925.

TEST MATCHES
Played in 12 Tests
BATTING – 16 inns, 5 not outs, 154 runs, 50* h.s., 14.00 ave. 4 catches.
BOWLING – 3732 balls, 1707 runs, 66 wkts, 25.86 ave., 3 'tens,' 5 'fives.'
Best performances:
12-171 v. South Africa, Manchester, 1929
10-93 v. West Indies, Manchester, 1928
10-207 v. South Africa, Leeds, 1929
Shared a partnership of 128 for 9th wkt with F. E. Woolley v. Australia, Sydney, 1924–25

RECORDS

3151 wickets in County Championship matches, exceeds Rhodes' 3112 wickets.

188 wickets/season during career, exceeds second highest of Colin Blythe, another great Kent bowler, by 42 wickets/season.

2090 wickets in 8 seasons – 1928 to 1935.

1122 wickets in 4 seasons – 1928 to 1931

12234 balls bowled in 1933; 11857 in 1928; 11487 in 1930 – the only occasions in excess of 11200.

5489 runs conceded in 1928 – only time a bowler has given over 5000 runs.

Three times he took all 10 wickets in an innings.

Only player ever to take over 300 wickets in a season (304 – 1928).

Only player ever to take 200 wickets by Aug. 14, reaching this total by July 27th in 1928, Aug. 1st in 1931, Aug. 6th in 1930, Aug. 7th in 1929 and Aug. 14th in 1933.

MISCELLANIA

1922 v. Sussex took 6-35, 6-36, 9-11, 8-56, or 29 wkts for 138 runs, an unbelievable average of 4.74.

1923 v. Somerset took 9 wkts personally – 5 ct, 3 b, 1 lbw – in match.

1928 Eight separate players made catches off 'Tich's' bowling v. Leicester at Tonbridge.

1929 Ames made 54 dismissals (18 ct, 36 st) off 'Tich's' bowling during season.

1930 Ames made 55 dismissals (19 ct, 36 st) off 'Tich's' bowling during season.

1932 Ames made 39 stumpings off 'Tich's' bowling during season.

1933 Todd made 5 catches off 'Tich's' bowling v. Gloucester at Canterbury.

1935 Woolley made 22 catches off Freeman's bowling in season; he made at least one catch from 'Tich's' bowling in every season.

Index

140

Hearne, J. T. 25-6
Hearne, J. W. 15, 30, 33, 35, 36, 47, 49, 54, 55, 65
Hendren, E. P. 22, 30, 54, 77, 88, 95
Hendry 55
Higgins, J. B. 71
Higgs, Jim 4, 123
Hignell, A. 2
Hill-Wood 44
Hirst, G. 49, 129
Hitch 21
Hobbs, Jack 19-21, 27, 31, 38, 53, 54, 56, 66, 77, 88, 93, 96, 116, 128, 129
Hobbs, Robin 2, 3, 5, 124
Holding, M. A. 3
Holland (N. S. W.) 4
Hollies, Eric 121, 122, 123
Holmes E. R. T. 83
Hooker, H. A. 15
Hourn, D. W. 4
Howell (Oxford U.) 19
Howell (Surrey) 27
Howell (Warwicks) 54, 55
Howlett 26
Hubble 70, 111
Huish 17, 19, 22, 85
Humphreys 18, 19, 111
Hutchings 24
Hutton, Len 122

Intikhab Alam 2, 35, 123, 124
Inverarity, M. 55
Inverarity, R. J. 55

Jackson, G. R. 73
Jameson, Capt 35
Jardine, D. R. 77, 92, 93, 95
Javed Miandad 2
Jeacocke 35
Jeeves 22
Jenkins, R. 123
Johnson, Ian 123
Johnston, Bill 123
Jupp, V. W. C. 34, 43, 78

Kallicharran, A. I. 2, 3
Kelleway 93, 95
Kennedy 29, 35, 42
Kent C. C. C. (Champions, 1913) 17
  v Surrey, 1914, Blackheath 19
  v Surrey, 1914, Lord's 20-1
  v Surrey, 1919, Oval 27

Kent C. C. C. (Champions, 1913) *cont.*
  v Middlesex, 1920, Canterbury 30
  v Surrey, 1922 30
  v Sussex, 1922 39-40
  v Middlesex, 1923 (Freeman knocked out)
  tour of Scotland, 1923, - 48. 1925-68
  v Northants, 1926 70
  v Hampshire, 1927 72-3
  v West Indies, 1928 83
  v Australians, 1930 110
  v Lancashire, 1932 114
  v Warwickshire, 1932 114
  v Yorkshire, 1933 116
Kidde, E. L. 35
Kilner 45, 50, 54, 57, 65
Kinneir (Warwicks) 22
Kippax 53, 95
Kirsten 1
Knight, D. J. 19, 22 ,31
Knight, A. E. 125

Laker, J. C. 40, 71, 123
Larwood, H. 78, 96, 106, 129
Latchman, H. 124
l. b. w. (''new'' law) 120
Leadbeater 123
Lee, G. M. 31
Lee, H. W. 25, 30
Leveson-Gower 46, 105
Levett, W. H. V. 13, 14, 22, 89, 117, 126, 127
Lewis 14
Leyland, M. 77, 94, 106
Lillywhite, W. 81
Lindwall, R. 123
Lockwood 12
Lohmann, G. A. 81
Lowry, T. C. 42, 44
Lyon, M. D. 54
Lyttleton, R. H. 29

Macartney 44, 93
Macaulay, G. 42, 45, 51
MacLaren, A. 10, 42, 43
Maclean 44
Mailey, Arthur 4, 15, 32, 36, 43, 49, 65, 93, 108, 122, 123
Mann, F. T. 30, 41, 83, 105
Marriott, C. S. 9, 28, 35, 48, 69, 90, 98, 100, 112, 116, 117, 121, 122, 127